CW00871921

Pathways to Lasting Self-Esteem

by

Stanley J. Gross, Ed. D.

authorHOUSE

1663 LIBERTY DRIVE, SUITE 200
BLOOMINGTON, INDIANA 47403
(800) 839-8640
www.authorhouse.com

First published by AuthorHouse 09/07/04

ISBN: 1-4184-7024-4 (e)
ISBN: 1-4184-7023-6 (sc)

Library of Congress Control Number: 2004094582

This book is printed on acid-free paper.

Printed in the United States of America
Bloomington, Indiana

When we run away from ghosts, they follow us.
When we stop and face them, they disappear.
Old Irish Saying

Dedicated to the memory of

Toby Theodore Doliner
1928-1973

"He glittered when he walked."
Edward Arlington Robinson

Table of Contents

Part III
Self-Care and Self-Esteem

Part IV
Slow Impulsive Responding

Part V
Transformation

Diagrams

ACKNOWLEDGMENTS

My debt to the late Virginia Satir is profound. I may never be wholly clear about all the ways she influenced me. Training with her was deeply instructive and inspiring. She was personally instrumental in the work I did on myself that resulted in the great leap forward my own self-esteem took. I make clear in the body of the book the concepts that derive from her work.[1]

I read the book, *Self-esteem: Paradoxes and Innovations in Clinical Theory and Practice*,[2] at a crucial time. It contributed the vital clarification that self-esteem develops as the result of facing our fears. Robert Firestone's *Compassionate Child Rearing* and Alice Miller's, *For Your Own Good* documented for me the culturally institutionalized cruelty directed at children in the name of parenting. These books normalized the widespread abuse and neglect we see and serve as the basis for the problems many of us have in living.

I thank Bunny Duhl for her off hand, but elegant explanation that the responsibility children take for everything that happens in their world comes from seeing themselves at its center. Sarah Stewart's seminar on dissociation clarified the nature of trance phenomena for me. Howard Schafer's invitation to join the visiting scholar's program at Harvard

---

[1] See *The New People Making* and *The Satir model*.
[2] Bednar, R. L., Wells, M. G., & Peterson, S. R. (1989). *Self-Esteem: Paradoxes and Innovation in Clinical Theory and Practice*. Washington, DC: American Psychological Association.

Medical School's Center for Addiction Study was my introduction to years of creative and meaningful work, first in addiction and later in self-esteem. Ellen Lewis and Lu Klimm at Alcohol Family Rehabilitation in Plymouth, MA eased my transition into doing this work.

I enjoyed sharing many of these ideas at the Boston Center for Adult Education and the Massachusetts School of Professional Psychology. Joyce Kuzmin deserves kudos for editing earlier portions of the book. Andy Horne and Brian Cartwright helped to sharpen its focus. Ben Fox's artful advice came at a crucial time. I thank Stephanie Nichols for her help and advice at crucial moments. I appreciate the skillful final editing by Marianne Galvin. I so cherish my wife, Julie McVay whose support is so special and who reads my musings with her pencil ever ready to clarify my prose.

The book is dedicated to my dear cousin Toby. My brother in spirit; we shared a family of origin, the joys and challenges of an expanding world, and supported each other through the pain of our own lack of readiness. His final gift to me was courage; he died as he had lived, taking chances.

This book contains observations from my personal and professional experience about what stimulates and sustains growth in self-esteem. I have been deeply influenced by my clients whose persistence and guts, teach me every day. I thank them, especially those who unknowingly contributed to the disguised vignettes that illustrate concepts in this book. Having seen the model work, I am optimistic about the possibilities for change and the existence of choice. Having struggled,

I am also cautious about the potential pitfalls, snares, and delusions. What follows can be both exciting and scary. It can also be the most important work anyone will ever do. Welcome to my roller coaster!

INTRODUCTION

Many of us are perplexed by the continuing struggle to raise self-esteem. We find it difficult to improve it even when motivated to do so. We've tried one way to change after another only to find effectiveness fade or enthusiasm wane. Emotional pain leads us to yearn for change, but change creates a confusion we fear. Our life experience has been a repeated avoidance of the daily stressful events we need to face. Instead, we have buried our energy in addiction and other harmful or self-defeating habits. A more durable and positive self-esteem seems just out of reach for want of knowing how to pursue it.

Pathways to Lasting Self-Esteem is designed to make an enduring impact. If you are like millions of others, you have tried, but not succeeded in gaining that needed breakthrough. This book is a response to that desire. The book distinguishes between the deeper work that must be done to raise global self-esteem from the more superficial manipulations commonly ineffective in making a lasting impact. *Pathways to Lasting Self-Esteem* acknowledges the tenacity of low self-esteem yet affirms that much can be done to raise it. It clarifies the nature of self-esteem and the ways to make something positive and lasting happen. The book offers hope to counter despair and safe options to offset fears.

What You Will Find Here

- <u>Why low self-esteem is so widespread in our society</u>: The abuse and neglect people experience in childhood lays the basis for low self-esteem. Even with minor forms of abuse and neglect, children who are not allowed to talk about their experience interpret negative events as their fault. The result is thinking they are wrong or bad or unwanted. These beliefs are kept secret and are responsible for a life-long habit of avoiding the fear evoked by negatively tinged events. Fear avoidance is the active ingredient in maintaining low self-esteem. Gaining positive self-esteem means facing the fears associated with our personal history of low self-esteem.

- <u>Facing fear raises self-esteem</u>: Two involuntary ways people avoid fear are described in this book. The *coping impulse trance* is an automatic response to fearful incidents, so that we fail to learn from them. *Insufficient skills* result from this avoidance and explain why we do not develop better skills to respond to common stressful events. By facing our fears, the trance can be slowed, and the skills can be gained to make lasting self-esteem a reality.

- <u>Stepwise skills developed to face fears</u>: We work through the following tasks at each of four levels. (Level ❶ represents low self-esteem.) The tasks at each level need to be solved before going on to the next level.

Level ❷ – Contain addictions and destructive habits via self-care, distraction, and group support.

Level ❸ – Select from a variety of self-caring options to create a success prophecy and validate positive self-esteem.

Level ❹ – Notice and acknowledge negative beliefs and impulsive acts to slow automatic responses to stressful events and stimulate effective action.

Level ❺ – Face resentment over the traumas of childhood to open the door to self-forgiveness and positive self-esteem.

Understanding the process of change and the roles of hope and safety help negotiate a procedure that can be confusing at times. You may find it useful, as I did, to know that self-esteem shares confusion with other desirable conditions – wisdom, happiness, and peace – as a common starting point. My grandfather told me many years ago, "Confusion is the source of all wisdom." This esteem raising process gives us choices about our ending point.

How I Developed These Ideas

It sometimes feels as if I have been exploring the concept of self-esteem all of my life. Several years ago I completed a period of advanced training with family therapy pioneer Virginia Satir. Self-esteem was the cornerstone of her work. I spent several subsequent years considering the relevance of her model to my work as a university professor of counseling psychology. I experimented with it in my teaching and in the groups I led.

After retirement from my university position and more retraining in substance abuse and family therapy, I began work as a consulting psychologist in an alcoholism clinic. Later, I opened a private psychotherapy practice. At first my clients were alcoholics in recovery or their partners and adult children. My practice broadened to include people struggling with a variety of problems in living. They sought to end the havoc caused by emotional distress. Most were willing to do the hard work necessary but had difficulty with the self-blaming and confusion accompanying awareness of their feelings. They repeatedly asked, "What should I do?" They did not appear to have skills to avoid or to solve their problems or they did not use the skills they had. Self-care was a recurrent issue. Many believed difficult situations pursued them or they could not say "no" to abuse. Some clients were being abused by their partners or other family members.

A pattern emerged featuring confusion as the starting point. Confusion frightened my clients. They seemed unable to deal with it on their own, relying instead on impulsive acts that usually turned out to be self-defeating or self-destructive. These impulsive acts were their attempt to control the nature of their experience. When they were stressed, their adult skills disappeared – repeatedly displaced by these impulsive responses. They did not know how to give up a control-oriented lifestyle for one relying on their inner strength.

Avoiding "disease" and moralistic explanations that some posit for addictive behavior, I could see my clients had no conscious control over their urgent response. When certain stressful events occurred it seemed an internal switch was thrown. They became defensive where previously they had been receptive. Descriptions of how they made decisions in their lives bore out the automatic character of their response to stress. They usually could not report the reasons for their impulsive actions. Though it did relieve the tension of the moment, their action often had a self-defeating down side. Even if they later acknowledged responsibility for their actions, stress would repeatedly pre-empt their clarity when the same situation reoccurred. Nor did they learn from their experience! Often addictive or obsessive behavior would follow the incident. Frequently, they were appealingly "sorry." It seemed to me that their loss of choice had a complexity beyond a simple a loss of skills. They did not appear to have a choice in the same sense as having options in a voting booth or in deciding when to cross a busy street. It appeared genuinely "mindless." How could I explain the basis for what I was seeing? I had experiences with two clients that helped me to clarify what I saw.

Barry was a 38 year-old recovering alcoholic with five years of sobriety. He had suffered severe physical abuse from his father in childhood. He came to see me because of difficulty in close relationships. As we talked about a recent rejection, I observed his eyes become glazed. He then looked away and changed the subject. When I asked him to return to the subject, he did not remember what he had said previously. I compared these reactions to those of other clients who would suddenly become unresponsive, engage in repetitive, barely relevant monologues, or be unable to maintain eye contact. It struck me that I had just observed a *trance* state. Talking about rejection stimulated his memory of childhood physical abuse.

This triggered confusion, which then cued his trance reaction. The trance worked to block his memory of childhood physical abuse and distanced him emotionally from its reenactment. I later labeled the loss of choice I had observed a *coping impulse trance*. The trance was the mechanism by which Barry kept the impact of his father's abuse away from himself.

This notion about trance led me to the psychological concept of dissociation, the mental process of "separating off" painful memories from conscious awareness. A trance is a mild dissociative experience induced by stress or trauma. My clients' confusion would become disconnected from its historical roots in childhood experience. The trances contained repetitive and automatic behavior, rendering their memory of traumatic events highly resistant to change. When impulsivity led to self-defeating action, my clients were unable to connect their actions to the consequences. Others were remorseful, feeling incapable of stopping themselves.

One of my first clients at the alcoholism clinic helped me to connect my observations of coping impulse trances to self-esteem. Cheryl was a 29-year-old woman and child of an alcoholic. She began our second session saying, "Well, I did it." Upon my asking what she did, she replied by telling me she had ended her sexual relationship with her married lover. It turned out that her awareness of her shame about their relationship (which she had not referred to in our first session) led her to see it as abusive. Perhaps, the discussion in our first session about saying "no" to her emotionally abusive mother had suggested her positive action. Whatever the reason, it represented her first step in establishing herself as a person separate from her mother and her lover. Her progress during the next few months was somewhat more complicated, but saying "no" to her lover and "yes" to herself was a crucial beginning.

This incident led me to connect the lack of a clear sense of boundaries to low self-esteem. Who could learn to feel good about themselves while experiencing emotional, physical, or sexual abuse? Spurred by this awareness, I looked for and identified other associations with low self-esteem. My clients saw danger rather than opportunity when facing new or problem situations. They were unaware of other options for action. Instead, they thought about these situations in "all or none" categories. Their feelings frightened them rather than aided their problem solving. It was difficult for them to assert themselves. They were likely to be aggressive or manipulative in meeting their needs. They did not expect to see positive outcomes for their efforts, nor were they able to tolerate genuine emotional closeness.

They also had difficulty seeing themselves as whole persons. Rather, they focused on their deficiencies. When new or problematic incidents occurred, they reenacted conditions characteristic of their childhood, usually with self-punishing results. In these circumstances, they reflected as adults the limited abilities associated with their childhood. Often their responses reflected extremes in thinking, feeling, and action (for example, emotional flooding or absence of feeling, black and white thinking). Since these responses did not fit their current circumstances, the outcome was often self-defeating or self-destructive. When threatened by circumstances, they did not have the adult skills available to choose alternative action. I labeled these actions as representing *skill insufficiencies.*

Finally, two concepts emerged as the glue holding together this model of low self-esteem. Abuse and neglect are not enough in themselves to be responsible for the self-punishing nature of low self-esteem. The inability to talk about trauma at the time it occurs is what makes the abuse and neglect so influential. When a disaster occurs in our society, we usually rush in with counselors to help victims debrief the experience. By helping victims to process their horror and sense of responsibility, we hope to prevent the event from entering memory unrefined. Instead, we encourage victims to share their feelings about the experience. We support them. We tell them they are reacting normally to an awful situation. We insist they are not responsible for what happened. But this is not what happens for the most part when there is abuse and neglect of children. *Unprocessed* – the abuse and neglect enter memory unrefined. Since children see themselves as the centers of the universe and responsible for everything that happens within it, they misperceive events. *They come to believe they are responsible for their own abuse and neglect.* Misperceiving, they victimize themselves. Their subsequent self-defeating and self-destructive actions represent *re-victimization.*

Low self-esteem was a constant theme in our psychotherapy sessions because my clients frequently mentioned it. It is common to hear the term low self-esteem at A.C.O.A.[3] and Alcoholic Anonymous meetings as a synonym for self-loathing. I came to see

[3] Adult Children of Alcoholics

a relationship between the emotional issues of low self-esteem and recovery from addiction. As my work with these clients continued, their self-esteem became a measure of their progress in recovery. Their self-esteem was a metaphor for their level of emotional development.

I began writing earlier versions of this book for my clients in recovery. I wanted to make information about the process more accessible. I particularly hoped my writing would clarify their personal growth work in psychotherapy and in twelve-step groups. Very soon, however, I found the concepts applied to a wider population enduring psychological distress. This shifted my focus from recovery to self-esteem.

Relevance of This Approach to the Public

Many of my clients talked openly about their low self-esteem. Others were offended by any reference to it, feeling stigmatized by the label. Yet the symptoms were duplicated in both groups. I used similar techniques to treat both groups with a similar degree of success. In fact, those who acknowledged their low self-esteem seemed a step ahead of those who did not do so. This raises an issue, which I believe has wider implications for the treatment of psychological distress than is indicated by the label "low self-esteem." I retain the concept because there is therapeutic power in its use. There are problems as the term self-esteem has the limitation of any label. It says too little and infers too much. The public meaning attached to the term varies from the shameful to the trivial. Many are confused by the conflicting ways the topic is treated in the mass media. Low self-esteem is widespread, yet it is treated so superficially it can become a joke even to the discerning reader. Yet, the substantial number of self-help books on the topic suggests that it speaks to a yearning by the public to better understand themselves. Finally, mistaken childhood beliefs perpetuated by low self-esteem allow important adult decisions (for example, marriage, career, and friendships) to be skewed by criteria that no longer fit.

Relevance of This Approach to Professionals

Psychotherapists vary in how they view self-esteem. Many enrolling in the workshops I lead tell me they are intrigued. They say that self-esteem is a widely used term in their clinical discussions, but its meaning is unclear. Others consider it superficial or a cult term, not worth serious consideration. In this way a readily available professional literature on self-esteem is ignored. What some professionals miss, to the detriment of the public they serve, is the part this literature plays in alleviating distress. My book advances this literature. It presents a clear model based on clinical observation and treatment experience that can help individuals develop emotionally and deal with their problems.

Further, my book uses an eclectic approach. It recasts existing knowledge and technique into a more accessible format. Several sources of psychotherapy theory are involved. The trance concept has its roots in dissociation, while restating some psychoanalytic ideas. The focus on skills is based in behavioral psychology. The centrality of mistaken core beliefs draws from cognitive therapy. The structure of roles, rules, and core beliefs is based on system concepts. The focus on awareness came from humanistic and Eastern roots. My work makes these therapeutic approaches available in a context of acceptance, transcending pathology, judgment, and shame. It offers to clients and therapists alike a stimulating hierarchy of challenges. In all, these present a road map for emotional growth.

Can I Change on My Own?

"Can I change on my own or do I need the help of a professional?" The answer to this question depends, in large part, on the reader's attitudes and skills. Wanting "magic," depending on others to solve one's problems, limited appreciation of psychological processes, and little curiosity about self all represent expectations that sabotage self-change. The following questions indicate some of the coping skills central to successful intentional change:

- How much do you want to learn about yourself?
- Do you have a record of persistence in self-learning?
- Do you have the staying power for the hard work of containing addictions and increasing self-care?
- Would you use help from friends, mentors, support groups, self-help books, and Internet resources?
- Are you curious?
- How open are you to hearing and incorporating feedback about your actions?
- How uneasy are you when confused?

Change issues are often very deeply personal and confusing. Defensiveness and avoidance block or distort awareness. Consulting with a professional would be advisable, if your defensiveness or avoidance blocks change. If you can use information about yourself to make changes, a psychotherapist or a coach might only be helpful some of the time or not at all. One way to find out is to use the techniques discussed in this book. If you achieve necessary changes, then you have answered your question. If you find that after trying several strategies and techniques you are still stuck, then you have another answer.

I offer three uses of this book for persons with low self-esteem. Some will be able to use the book as a principal guide with only the help of friends and support groups to make appropriate changes. Some will use the book as an important resource but occasionally employ psychotherapy or coaching. Finally, some will use the book as secondary resource but rely on psychotherapy or coaching. The book will also be useful to psychotherapists and coaches to clarify a model of change to increase self-esteem.

If You Decide to Work on Your Own

You may find certain ideas in this book confusing. No doubt, it may appear complicated at times. New ideas often do, at first. Don't let that put you off. Since this is a step-by-step program, consider that confusion lets you know you've just gotten ahead of yourself. Take it one step at a time. Accepting this notion, you will be able to focus on the next step. When you feel some discomfort, turn to Chapter 10 for self-soothing options.

Plan of the Book

I have divided my book into five parts. Parts I and II include eight chapters, which cover topics about self-esteem and the process of intentional change. Part III includes initial steps in raising self-esteem – containing addiction and enhancing self-care. Part IV provides a way of slowing impulsiveness. Finally, Part V describes the process of transformation.

xxx

PART I

I don't know who I am.

DEFINING SELF-ESTEEM

Low self-esteem is as common as a head cold in the winter, a bloom in the spring, pollen in the summer, or leaves on the ground in the fall. Low self-esteem is not as evident as these events. Of them, it is most like pollen, which can't be seen, it must be inferred by a sneeze.

> *Peter wakes up feeling disgusted. Once again he drank too much the night before and has little memory of it. He resolves to limit himself to two drinks tonight, but he has stopped counting how many times he has made that vow.*

> *Susan feels her marriage is on autopilot since the birth of their six-month old twin girls. Five nights a week her husband goes to an AA meeting, missing the evening ritual with the children. She is angry that he does not care enough to be there. When he is home on the weekend, she goes shopping.*

> *Amos, ordinarily a loving father, is critical of his daughter Amy when she dawdles at dressing*

those mornings he gets her to nursery school. He feels such irritation and the words "just come out." Then he feels terrible.

Jean worries about being incompetent. She works hard and achieves, but when she is successful she chalks it up to luck or circumstance. She would like other people to acknowledge her ability but has a hard time hearing compliments when they do.

Robert is a successful stockbroker and frequenter of the "bar scene." Born in England, his natural charm, accent, and good looks make him attractive to women. These relationships begin with high hopes, but he soon gets bored. His fear of rejection and commitment interfere with his becoming involved with a woman capable of the more substantial relationship he yearns for.

These people have a shared secret*. It is dangerously near to becoming known. It comes up unbidden, like lava from a volcano when they feel the shame of low self-esteem. They react quickly to suppress it, but it is always there, ready to surface. Peter and Susan directly abuse themselves by addictive drinking and compulsive spending. Amos overreacts while Jean and Robert are following self-defeating paths. What they all have in common is the shame they know as

*Note: If you want to know the secret now, it is explained in Part IV. Due to the nature of the secret, it may not have much meaning until you have worked through Parts I, II, and III. Though I recommend you wait, you can turn to Chapter 13 for an explanation.

2

low self-esteem. The people in these vignettes will reappear though out this book to help explain things. To begin with, we will explore the meaning of the concept of self-esteem.

Stanley J.Gross, Ed. D.

Chapter 1

WHAT IS SELF-ESTEEM?

Low self-esteem develops unseen by the naked eye. It is fostered by negative beliefs about self. These beliefs grow from abuse and neglect suffered during childhood. A common fact of human experience, abuse and neglect are an important part of the setting of growing up. Viewing self-esteem as beginning in the context of the family turns self-esteem from being a personal problem of individuals to a social problem, which *affects* individuals. By normalizing the problem in this way we remove the stigma of low self-esteem from those individuals who are least equipped to handle it. Thus, we view the problem of low self-esteem as a *normal reaction to an abnormal situation.* Of course, people with low self-esteem have the responsibility to raise it, but this view locates the problem where it belongs.

Some abuse and neglect by caretakers is *unintentional.* Appropriate limits, stimulation, and positive regard for children may be absent or insufficient. There may be little awareness of the effects of denying to children these necessary conditions for growth (See Chapter 4). Robert Firestone's, *Compassionate Child Rearing* and Alice Miller's, *For Your Own Good* clearly describe the widespread institutionalized cruelty directed toward children. Examples include many beliefs and practices thought to be normal because they follow some social custom. Some believe it is appropriate to prefer boys to girls. Some invoke harsh discipline to teach respect. Some believe anger at obstinate or whining children changes behavior. Some encourage achievement over respect for a child's uniqueness. Some discourage experimentation for fear of failure.

Some of the abuse and neglect qualifies as *intentional.* These caretakers know what they are doing and either do not care, do not know the consequences of their acts, or are unable to stop their abusive or neglectful acts. Some of these parents believe they can't help themselves. Others find a social or religious reason to justify callous or ruthless behavior. Such abuse and neglect is often more extreme in aim, form, and effect. Reports of severe physical, sexual, and emotional abuse as well as serious deprivation and neglect are said to total in the millions yearly. Examples include: physical beatings, sexual abuse, lack of care, and raging.

It is not the purpose of this book to deal with the important social problem of neglect and abuse of children. I address it here at the beginning of this work so as not to lose sight of its source. This book is limited to clarifying the nature of low self-esteem and to providing clear pathways to a lasting and positive self-esteem.

DEFINING SELF-ESTEEM

For many, the term "self-esteem" is an overripe cliché or a joke. They often use the term with little idea of its meaning, yet it refers to a crucial dimension of our lives.

Self-esteem is the judgment we make about our worth as persons. This judgment relies on how well we "know ourselves." Self-knowledge results from our experience in facing life challenges, dilemmas, and fears. The more experience we have, the more we know, and the better we feel. We are more competent in facing life events; feel safer in our environment; and more hopeful about the future. Thus, self-esteem measures the effectiveness and the quality of our lives. But, like happiness or peace, self-esteem is a byproduct of how we live our life, not a goal in itself.

Self-esteem is a factor affecting general health as well as personal distress and emotional problems. It plays a part in competency and satisfaction in relationships as well as in productivity, morale, and stress at work. Though used a lot as a label, there is a great deal of confusion about its meaning. Unfortunately, the term is bandied about without much precision. One reason for this is that there are two types of self-appraisals involved. These judgments come from different points of view, but they are often talked about as if they are the same thing.

Global (lasting) Self-Esteem

Global self-esteem, the focus for this book, is an enduring self-appraisal based on one's degree of self-knowledge. This evaluation represents our understanding of "who we are." Global self-esteem grows as we face fears in our daily life. Facing fears allows us to develop self-confidence by learning from experience, gaining mastery over challenges and dilemmas, and reducing symptoms of personal distress. Developing such confidence permits us to be aware of our inner selves, thus we enhance our courage to continue to face our fears. Will Schutz (1994) in *The Human Element* says, "It is impossible to have high self-respect and self-liking without great self-awareness" (p. 99).

Avoidance of fear, on the other hand, blocks opportunities for learning about self, others, and the world at large. By avoiding fears, global self-esteem remains static. Recently, an 11-year-old wanted to know the difference between, "What I want to do and what my friends want me to do." The *Ask Beth* columnist in the *Boston Globe*[4] did a good job in defining global self-esteem in response. She advised her to pay attention to her feelings and to take time to figure out what she wanted. Then she added, "Learning to pay attention to yourself is the best way to develop good self-esteem."

Situational (momentary) Self-Esteem

Situational self-esteem has a different basis. It, too, is a self-appraisal, but it is based on our immediate social experience. For example, being invited to join a select group or getting a promotion at work might increase our situational self-esteem, since these events are usually experienced as validating. Most of us want to belong and achieve. Similarly, falling in love shows us how lovable we are. Failing to achieve at work or rejection by a loved one is likely to have the opposite effect. Situational self-esteem can shift quickly and radically following affirming or invalidating events. Because of this we may have positive self-esteem in some settings (for example, work, academics, or athletics because these setting

[4] November 11, 2003, p. F6.

are more structured and we get kudos there) but lower self-esteem in other areas of our lives (for example, our intimate relationships because of less structure and the influence of family values).

Several problems emerge from using situations to determine self-esteem. The changing nature of situational self-esteem encourages manipulation or denial of low global self-esteem. This occurs when we emphasize accomplishment and external rewards to the exclusion of knowing ourselves. We may dupe ourselves into thinking we have high self-esteem yet be plagued by anxiety or depression. Situational self-esteem also gives an unstable picture. One moment our situational self-esteem is high. Later, we find ourselves uncertain and disappointed. Situational self-esteem also generates superficial thinking, as in "teaching" self-esteem to schoolchildren or repeating self-valuing affirmations. These activities may have some limited positive value, but it is preposterous to think these techniques can raise self-esteem for very long.

This situational basis for self-esteem can reduce the self-esteem concept to public ridicule in some circles. Even professionals and researchers who rely on a situational definition of self-esteem can come to outrageous conclusions: "[P]eople with high self-esteem are more likely to act aggressively with others."[5] In this case the writers relied on subject self-report about their own self-esteem. Even more outrageous is an advertisement in the November 2002 *American Psychologist*. The ad describes a drug as, "[T]he science behind ADHD and self-esteem." Such

---

[5] *Psychotherapy Newsletter,* March/April 2002, pp. 16-17.

simplistic views undermine genuine efforts to attend to the root causes of low global self-esteem in the abuse and neglect of children.

Positive Global Self-Esteem

Positive global self-esteem is an affirmative self-judgment of our worth. Positive global self-esteem is not just a "feel good" state. It means we have enough self-knowledge to understand our needs and "who we are." We believe in ourselves, and we are diligent about self-care. This self-knowledge is essential to becoming more fully human, dealing with life's problems, and developing respectful and loving relationships. We have confidence in our intuitive inner voice. This confidence is a result of our willingness to face life as it is; to be open to change when necessary; to accept meaningful achievement; to receive support from others; to take assertive action; and to learn from experience.

Low Global Self-Esteem

Low global self-esteem is our negative self-judgment of worth. We are pessimistic about our options and our futures. We worry about our abilities and what others think of us. We take an impulsive approach to stress and problem solving. We fail to care for ourselves and allow abuse by others. We isolate or have superficial relationships. We fear even reasonable risks or recklessly take extraordinary risks. Low self-esteem expresses itself in shame, self-doubt, inadequacy, aggression, arrogance, and even denial that these thoughts exist. By avoiding fear, our absence of self-knowledge has us say, "I don't know who I am." Low global self-esteem increases vulnerability to emotional distress, anxiety, depression, stress, and addiction.

Low self-esteem is characterized by insufficient skill in six areas or domains (See Chapter 12). It can be recognized as prominently featuring one or more of the following characteristics:

- Impulse-driven actions include substance abuse and compulsive habits with self-destructive results or blocked action.

- Emotional uncertainty where lack of self-knowledge results in disruptive or blocked feelings.

- Dualistic thinking where either/or considerations restrict options and choice.

- Fused or aloof relationships foster abuse, poor self-care, and people pleasing.

- Control needs lead to self-defeating, dominating, manipulative, and submissive action.

- Self-absorbed or worry about externals sparks distortion or blocking the reception of new information.

LEVELS OF SELF-ESTEEM

Global self-esteem exists on five levels. Our degree of personal skill in dealing with life's dilemmas distinguishes one level from another. These skill levels are progressive in the sense that we grow from insufficiency of skill to increasing skill sufficiency.

Lower level skills are to be achieved before we are able to approach higher-level skill. These skill levels represent our increasing ability to deal with our fears of confusion, stress, and change in a way that leads to growth and competence. As we grow, we learn to "know ourselves." We gradually gain the sense of comfort, safety, hope, and inner control we know as positive self-esteem.

LEVEL ❶ On this level we abuse ourselves via substance addiction or dependence on compulsive habits. These habits include: codependency, sexual and relationship "addictions," spending compulsions, binge eating, gambling, work-a-holism, and raging. We are impulsive, negative, and look outside ourselves for things to change. Addictions and dependencies block awareness of fear and absorb energy to change. We do not believe that our skills are sufficient to face our fears.

LEVEL ❷ This level is the beginning of our ability to grow a more positive self-esteem. Here we face the fear of substituting self-care for the addictive substance or habit. Expect cravings for substances or destructive habits to increase in the short term. We experience both wanting to contain our habits as well as wanting to return to them. Learning to deal with the cravings is the challenge at this level. Admitting our role in the problem, developing a plan using self-care, self-soothing, distraction, reaching out for support, and learning sobriety and relapse prevention skills help us to tip the balance in favor of containment. It also permits us to work effectively at the next level where we learn to incorporate other self-caring practices into our life.

LEVEL ❸ By adopting self-affirming actions, cravings are a less common experience. These positive actions include such activities as exercise and a healthy diet. Figuring out how to maintain self-caring activities is the challenge at this level.

LEVEL ❹ Here we tackle our impulsive personalizing of stressful events. We see how impulses block our ability to face our fear of confusion, stress, and change. We gain tools and skills to slow our impulses. Addressing the negative beliefs at the core of our over reactions is the challenge at this level. As a result, we reduce our personalizing of negative events. This improves our ability to act in more positive and affirming ways. Becoming aware of the consequences of our choices, we learn about ourselves, whether or not our actions succeed or fail.

LEVEL ❺ On this level we exchange our negative and pessimistic view of ourselves for one that is more positive and affirming. We now have an active involvement in self-care and the ability to slow our impulsive responses to stress. This gives us a heightened access to our inner resources and allows us to deal effectively with life's dilemmas. The challenge at this level is to restore the lost historical connections between childhood abuse and neglect for which we took responsibility, on one hand, and our mistaken negative core beliefs, on the other. Changes do not occur overnight. A sustained process of facing our fears and learning about our grief over the loss of childhood will make the difference.

IMPACT OF LOW GLOBAL SELF-ESTEEM

Avoiding fear blocks learning important life lessons about ourselves, about other people, and about the world around us. This means we are not prepared to deal effectively with stress or consider varied solutions to life issues. Instead, we repeatedly respond impulsively and ineffectively. We don't develop new skills to improve our response. Thus, new and scary events continually result in self-defeating or self-destructive action.

For some of us, the combination of lack of readiness to deal with stress and a lifetime of self-punishment is devastating. We are so damaged by being abused or neglected we focus on protecting ourselves at all costs. This greatly reduces our vulnerability but, in doing so, we succumb to self-abusive life strategies. We hurt and violate others, medicate our distress with addiction or dependency, distort our experience in mental illness, or by neglecting self-care become physically debilitated. We may, in the words of the poet, pursue "lives of quiet desperation" in which our low self-esteem periodically causes us to be irritable, miserable, conflicted, and/or ineffective.

Severe abuse and neglect are not the only conditions yielding low global self-esteem. A parent's negative criticisms, put downs, unrealistic expectations, over protection, or over indulgence can also have a lasting negative impact. Children exposed to such caretaker behavior who did not have an opportunity to talk about their feelings as young children will also protect their

14

vulnerability with over-sensitivity to life challenges. They, too, will fear negative events and stress. They, too, will respond with less serious but still self-defeating and self-destructive behaviors. They, too, will have learned to doubt themselves and respond impulsively to anything they find threatening.

SUBSEQUENT EFFECTS OF LOW SELF-ESTEEM

The first major effect of low self-esteem is the absence of a conscious choice when impulses direct our actions. In this case, we neither have an awareness of an alternative to what we do repeatedly, nor do we learn anything from this dysfunctional behavior. So when people say, "I didn't know what else to do" or "I couldn't help it," these statements are true in their view. Though, this does not excuse abusive behavior, for example, it does explain why people repeatedly act in self-defeating ways that hurt others or themselves.

By acting impulsively people avoid the natural lessons that come from dealing with stressful circumstances. As a result, they fail to develop the skills we all need to deal with such events. When stressful events occur, we neither know to choose, how to choose, or what to choose. A sense of helplessness and hopelessness prompts us to ask, "What should I do?" Lacking these skills, we do not even know what to do with any advice we may hear. In this way, we repeatedly maintain our ineffective behavior.

Having had to fend off a mix of neglect, indifference, and abuse in our childhood, we do not learn essential life skills when it is appropriate to do so. We are too busy just coping. Later, as adults, new or problem incidents continue to foster reenactments of childhood abuse or neglect. Our responses reflect a continuing lack of skill to deal with particular life stresses. Our feelings frighten us rather than aid problem solving. We see danger rather than opportunity when facing new or problem situations. When stressed we are unaware of other options. Instead, we think about these situations in dogmatic and option-limiting "all or none" categories. We have difficulty asserting ourselves and instead tend to be either submissive or aggressive in our relations with others. We worry a lot and do not expect to see positive outcomes for our efforts. Our boundaries are unclear, so we allow others to abuse us, we abuse ourselves, and we ignore self-care. We tend to be self-absorbed, isolated, and unreceptive to others while needing them at the same time. In the following, Jean's great need for approval dominates her decision-making and distorts her life.

Jean doesn't think of herself as having a self-esteem problem. If she thought about it at all she might say, "Low self-esteem is for people who want an excuse for not achieving." And achieve she does. She works very hard at her job as an accountant. Her co-workers call her a workaholic. She is extremely competent at her work and confident to the edge of arrogance with her co-workers.

Jean is an only child of parents who married late. She was born when they were in their late thirties. Both her mother and father were college professors who treated her kindly, but as if she were a student who wanted feedback on her actions. They were often busy preparing for classes and with their scholarly work, so they had little time for Jean's activities. Sometimes, Jean thought she was invisible to them.

Jean grew up anxious to please her parents. She was an excellent student in school and college and made partner in her accounting firm in her early thirties. Yet she never felt she received her parents' approval for these achievements and now she gets no pleasure from the compliments that come her way. Though still wanting approval, she passes off praise to focus on the next challenge. She does not understand what keeps her from enjoying the fruits of her efforts and what blocks her from more comfortable relations with others. She is lonely and wants to be involved in relationships, yet judges the men she meets as slackers.

Chapter 2

HOW WE MAINTAIN LOW SELF-ESTEEM

We grow emotionally by meeting life's daily challenges. Though we may become adults chronologically, we do not grow in physical, intellectual, or emotional functioning without learning from the variety of tests we face in growing up. Tests such as how to throw a ball, write a sentence, deal with a bully, or run a cash register are met daily on the athletic field, in the neighborhood, in schools and colleges, amongst our peers, at our jobs, and in our families. In each of these situations, the challenges and dilemmas have the potential to teach us about our environment, our needs, and how to make our way in the world. The extent to which we take advantage of these opportunities makes all the difference.

Often these challenges and dilemmas are confusing and uncomfortable. When we do not have needed coping skills and emotional support, we may become so fearful that we see these challenges as threats to our integrity as persons. These threats may produce fears about personal loss, our lack of ability, or our inadequacy. When we face these fears, we open up the possibility of learning about them and ourselves. In this way we increase our self-knowledge and our self-esteem. If we avoid facing these fears, we sidestep this learning and maintain our low self-esteem.

18

The Low Self-Esteem Cul-de-Sac

By slowing down the process of reaction we become able to see its separate parts and begin to understand how to change. Diagram # 1 describes the cul-de-sac.

1. **Certain social demands or new experiences** – An event we see as a demand or a challenge starts things off. If the demand is familiar, we probably have the required physical resources, coping skills, and/or emotional support to deal with it. If we believe these resources exist, the dilemma will not seem so scary. Rather, it will be seen as an opportunity to learn something. In that case, the arousal feels more like excitement than fear, setting up action to deal with the dilemma. Positive self-esteem results from efforts to face the challenge. Often, however, the event is not familiar nor do we have the requisite skill or support

2. **Situation threatens personal safety** – The lack of familiarity and the absence of skill and support stir concern that we do not know how to respond to the event. We have a dilemma! Ordinarily, we don't like dilemmas. Dilemmas make us uncomfortable because they threaten our feeling of safety.

3. **Situation unfamiliar and confusing** – When we are threatened by the new or unfamiliar, we become confused. The confusion triggers fear. We are concerned that our worst fears will come true immediately. We believe we do not have needed emotional support, physical resources, or coping skill to deal with this situation.

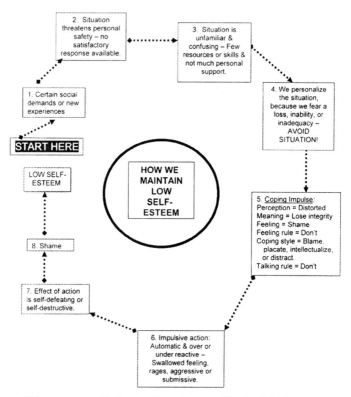

Diagram # 1 – The Low Self-Esteem Cul-de-Sac

4. **We personalize the situation** – We believe we do not know how to deal with the challenge. We fear our integrity will be compromised. The meaning we give to the situation creates a sense of vulnerability (for example, believing that the event occurred because we are "wrong" or "bad" or inadequate in some way). By personalizing the dilemma, we muster our defenses against attack. Increased activity and narrowing of attention gear us up to deal with the threat. We experience increased heart rate, fast and shallow breathing, perspiration, increased muscle tension, and a drop in temperature in our extremities. We respond in an automatic and habitual way to rid ourselves of this discomfort.

5. **Coping impulse** – Our response to threat comes in the form of a trance. It follows a pattern. It is automatic. As a habit, we are unaware of its role in protecting us from the threat. The coping impulse trance has six characteristics noted in Diagram 1. The trance state is more fully described in Chapter 11.

6. **Impulsive action** – We act to control some aspect of our environment or our reaction to it in order to avoid the fear. This may involve swallowing our feelings; raging explosively at a "tormentor;" or by resorting to an addiction to block our feelings. These automatic responses have adaptive value (that is, they do something *for* us) otherwise they would not persist. Derived from the "fight or flight" response, they represent a way we protect ourselves. Since the necessity for this emergency response is relatively rare in our modern society,

we act as if there is an emergency when there is none.

7. **Effect of action** – In attempting to control we lose control. Our actions usually are self-defeating or self-destructive. That is, they seem to control things but do not reassure us and may wind up hurting us. When the arousal passes, we may regret the action but don't believe we could have avoided it.

8. **Shame** – The experience confirms our low self-esteem. It leaves us with a sense of shame and erodes any belief in ourselves we may have entertained.

In the following, Robert's inability to face his fear of rejection has him persisting in a lifestyle that runs counter to his desire for a long-term relationship. Though fear is close to the surface, his mindless social activity blocks him from confronting its self-defeating nature, so he never risks or learns what blocks the realization of his yearning.

> *Robert is a successful stockbroker. He is unmarried, forty years of age, and a "babe magnet." His social life is a continuing round of short-term sexual encounters with much younger women. He feels trapped by this lifestyle when he meets friends who are in long-term relationships. He has a yearning he explains away as "too romantic." He tells himself it is not for him, but a shameful sense of unlovability persists.*

Robert is the youngest of six children from an emotionally abusive and chaotic family. His older siblings viewed him as the favorite of his inconsistent parents. These siblings were nice to him when his parents were around and rejecting when they were not. He learned early that when he pleased others they were less harsh with him and he could get what he wanted from them. Abuse, however, would come "out of the blue" so he was never certain of his standing with his parents or his siblings. He decided as a teen-ager to get as far away from his family as he could and emigrated to the U.S. after completing his undergraduate degree.

Robert maintains his low self-esteem without awareness of his contribution, which is opposed to what he says he wants. This is a too-common story.

Chapter 3

VISUALIZING "SELF"

Misunderstandings about positive self-esteem define it as a state of blissful happiness or rampant self-congratulation. Such misinterpretations have, in turn, subjected the concept to ridicule. Our meaning here should be clear – with increased self-esteem we become *more of ourselves*, not someone different. However, we then raise the question, what do we mean by *ourselves*?" Further, what do we mean by "self?"

The self contains the many aspects of our life experience. The self comprises our <u>identity</u> and the <u>roles</u> we take in life. Identity represents our uniqueness as a person and our sameness over time and circumstance. Identity develops as we experiment, choose, and reflect on the series of life challenges we encounter while growing up. Growth in identity may involve confusion, pain, as well as acute awareness. Growth can be stifled by highly restrictive settings, rigid beliefs, inflexible practices as well as addictive and habitual behavior. As identity develops we become more aware. We learn who we are, the choices available to us, how to choose, and how our society determines roles for us. We can choose when to follow our own "distant drummer" or the advice of our social groups.

Roles are the scripts or expectations attached to the various positions (for example, daughter, hero) or parts we play in our life with others. Roles comprise the contexts in which situational self-esteem is influenced. The scripts or expectations for these parts are usually unwritten but widely known. (See Chapter 13)

THE SELF-ESTEEM MANDALA

The self is far more complicated than can be described in any model of it. My adaptation of Virginia Satir's, "Self Mandala"[6] introduces the concept of self by using the Mandala as an example (See Diagram # 2). The Mandala is an ancient Buddhist design representing the ebb and flow of life. The Buddhist tradition uses the Mandala as a tool for a meditative ritual to enhance healing and transformation. Swiss psychiatrist Carl Jung introduced the concept into Western culture to describe his own and his patients' circle drawings that he associated with the self.

Many find the Mandala unsettling upon first encountering it. Trungpa titles his book on the Mandala, *Orderly Chaos.* He asserts that the Mandala has a pattern, but it is confusing to work with the pattern. It is worth it he says, since, "The idea of enlightenment is born out of confusion."[7]

The center of the self-esteem Mandala is surrounded by a combination of eight *dimensions* and six *realms.* The eight dimensions represent constant aspects of our life experience. The dimensions include:

---

[6] Satir, V., Banmen, J., Gerber, J., & Gamori, M. (1991). *The Satir Model: Family Therapy and Beyond.* Palo Alto, CA: Science and Behavior Books, pp. 274-283.
[7] Trungpa, C. (1991). *Orderly Chaos.* Boston: Shambala. p. 4.

Stanley J.Gross, Ed. D.

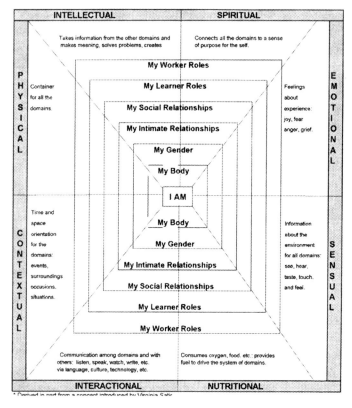

Diagram # 2 – Self-esteem Mandala

sensual, nutritional, interactional, contextual, physical, intellectual, spiritual, and emotional. In the structure of the Mandala, the dimensions interconnect. Changing one dimension creates a ripple effect among all the dimensions. Learning something new (intellectual) may cause us to be joyful (emotional).

The six realms refer to the separate arenas or settings in which we live our lives. These include: Body, gender, family, peers, school, and occupation. The realms close to the center represent early settings (time-wise) in the course of our lives, while those on the periphery represent later settings. For example, our experience in our family of origin precedes our school experience.

The Mandala in its entirety depicts our global self-esteem. The "I am" in the center has 48 sections surrounding it (six realms multiplied by eight dimensions). It interacts with the other rectangles to form an image of the self. Each of the 48 sections is made up of one dimension (for example, "sensual") and one realm (for example, "my gender"). This is a way to describe, "Who we are." Understanding how the dimensions and realms interact gives us clues to understand ourselves, our connections with others, and the world at large.

Examining the diagram, we note those sections unknown to us as well as those we know. Some sections are clearly associated with positive or low self-esteem. This explains how we can have high self-esteem sometimes but not other times. For example, we find the demands of work exciting; we function at a high level; and experience positive self-esteem in that realm of our lives. Later at home, we feel our life is going nowhere; we function at a low spiritual level; and rate our self-esteem accordingly. Or, we may feel good about our physical bodies but feel that our intimate relationships are a bust. Many actions draw upon two or more realms. Sexuality, for example expresses physical, sensual, emotional, and intellectual realms. The following eight dimensions follow Satir's[8] formulation.

THE DIMENSIONS

Sensual

Our sensual dimension includes our capacity to receive feedback about our actions and our impressions of the world around us – what we see, hear, taste, smell, and touch. The intellectual dimension of the Mandala takes data gathered by our senses and converts it into meaning. Sensory input may confuse us and distort our perception. Often people have a preference for some types of sensory awareness over others (for example, the visual over the auditory). We can be especially aware of some senses and filter out others. Smell is said to be our most suppressed sense. We may be unaware that we have not heard feedback in a social situation, so we miss learning needed information. Our self-esteem contributes to our interpretation of sensual phenomena. If we are negative, we may judge our slowness to react to new ideas as a deficiency. If we are positive, we may judge that we are cautious rather than slow.

[8] Satir, *et. al. Op. Cit.*

Nutritional

Our nutritional dimension takes in the fuel our body needs to flourish (for example, oxygen, food, and drink) and distributes it by converting it into energy. All systems need energy, and it comes in many forms (for example, blood sugar or adrenalin). When energy is toxic or insufficient, chaos can occur. All dimensions of the Mandala use energy and require it to maintain balance. What happens if some dimensions receive insufficient attention? Or, what if they become overloaded? Binge eating, for example represents over use of our nutritional dimension to substitute for emotional problems, causing us physical problems and the experience of shame and low self-esteem.

Interactional

Our interactional dimension refers to the ways we communicate – listening, speaking, watching, writing, and moving in space. A complex web of language, rules, technology, and physical resources affects how we interact. There are many blocks and distortions in communication, which affect our ability to understand and adapt to the circumstances of our lives. Rules learned in our families have an impact, for example, on expressing feeling and listening to others, creating openness or restraint in self-expression. People who are open in their self- expression would probably rate this aspect of their self-esteem as positive.

Contextual

Our contextual dimension includes the physical and social settings in which our lives play out. These are the situations, surroundings, events, occasions, rituals, and circumstances as well as our houses, jobs, cars, games, ceremonies, and toys. This is the dimension of the Mandala that tunes us into time and space. We learn to seek some contexts as well as which to avoid. The context is influential in affecting our actions; so we may be more comfortable in circumstances where expectations are clear. Depending on the clarity of the expectations, we may act appropriately or ineffectively. Familiarity is another attribute of context that some find comforting, and others find stifling. Each one of these circumstances can affect our experience of self-esteem.

Physical

Our anatomical body is the vessel in which we contain all the other dimensions of the Mandala. Our body connects with all the other dimensions to create an organism similar to other human organisms but unique in heredity and experience. Our body often seems to work automatically. It sends us complex messages by the sensations it emits, if we care to listen. Our body is also changing over time. Sometimes that surprises us. Other times we may be glad about it or resent it. Bodies come in various shapes and sizes. How we perceive our body may affect our sense of self-esteem. The color of our skin, our height, and our shape are aspects of our body subject to a variety of meanings. The energy of many people that goes into looking "beautiful" reveals the degree of importance of this dimension to situational self-esteem.

Intellectual

Our intellectual dimension is our ability to sustain thought, to reason, to learn, to derive meaning, and to use the information gathered by other dimensions of the Mandala. The intellectual includes our ability to think in a rational fashion, to solve dilemmas, and to dream of possibilities. We each have our way of processing information taken in by other dimensions. Some people are quite impulsive, while others are more restrained or thoughtful. Our awareness of our effectiveness in using this ability affects our self-esteem. Our ability to come up with a variety of problem-solving options to a perplexing dilemma would allow us to rate this dimension positively.

Spiritual

Our spiritual dimension can be our connection to a remote higher authority, to other beings, to the universe, or to a sense of purpose beyond the immediate. Every culture offers some types of spiritual opportunities. These are often ritualized in the great variety of formal and informal religions. These religions often honor humane purposes, connections to others or the environment, and the mystery of the universe. They may also divide humans and give birth to beliefs that foster separation, conflict, and oppression. A connection to other people in a spiritual setting is often viewed positively.

Emotional

Our emotional dimension refers to the feelings we have in reaction to the experiences of our lives: our joy, fear, anger, and grief. Feelings are always about something, thus they offer us information about our needs as we interact in our world. Our emotions serve much the same function as pain does in our physical body by helping us to live and survive in the world. Some feelings were so terrifying when we are small children that we may have learned to suppress or distort them. Family and cultural rules regulate expression of feelings. If we have learned that we were not supposed to express anger, for example, feeling this emotion might be accompanied by agitation.

The following vignette depicts how Diane and Wayne approach the emotional, physical, and interactional dimensions in their lives. Diane's awareness of the excessive emphasis on the sexual in their relationship reveals the absence of effective communication. Not knowing themselves, they experience difficulties in their emotional connection. They could discover more of "who they are", apart from their roles of husband (as good provider) and wife (as responsible for their relationship) by talking about their need for one another. Changing the way they interact could tune them into the spiritual, intellectual, and sensual dimensions of their lives. Doing so could impact favorably on the emotional, physical, and interactional dimensions of their relationship.

> *When Diane wanted to talk about her dissatisfaction with their relationship, Wayne left the room to watch TV. Later that evening he suggested they have sex. Diane, suppressing her anger, retreated into a book. He got her attention when he said; "You never want to have sex with me anymore." She replied, "You never listen to me anymore." To which he retorted, "It's always what you want." She responded, "You don't care about me. All you care about is a piece of ass."*

Diane interpreted Wayne's inattention and withdrawal as abandonment. She invests so much of herself in her relationship with Wayne that she does not know "who she is" when they do not connect. In the past she had allowed sex to be the way she experienced the connection, but, recently, her boredom with their relationship had her looking for more in how they communicated with each other. With her difficulty talking about her neediness, she interprets the problem as Wayne's indifference, blaming him for her dissatisfaction.

Wayne hears her blaming and acts to avoid a confrontation, which he knows will make him the goat. Always anxious to please others, he becomes confused and frightened when Diane criticizes him. He thought he loved her, but, lately, he has been eyeing other women and yearning to be with his single friends. He did not know what he wanted from their relationship, if it wasn't going to be sexual. After all, he was a good provider. He did not deserve Diane's anger, especially since she was not holding up her end of their bargain.

Chapter 4

ANTECEDENTS OF SELF-ESTEEM

Mary and Bill are both in their early 30s and have two school-age children. They argue frequently about doing household chores, managing Mary's anger, Bill's watching TV "all the time," and his weekly going out drinking with "the boys." Before their first child was born, their life was filled with work, family, friends, and a lot of partying. Mary has adapted to the changes children bring and resents the fact that Bill has not. They both have demanding jobs they must maintain to support their lifestyle. They do share transporting children to daycare and school. Otherwise, Bill does "fix up" around the house, mows the lawn, and tinkers with the car. He is indifferent to other household chores and childcare. He does not consider them as part of his role. He says he needs the TV and his "one night out a week" to relax.

Though stressed, Mary feels guilty about working and saddles herself with the major responsibility for the children, the housekeeping, and their relationship. Mary gets angry when she sees Bill watching TV while she is washing the dinner dishes or putting the children to bed. She resents his weekly Thursday night "appointment" with his childhood buddies but limits her own outside contacts to phoning old friends. She argues that Bill takes no responsibility for pulling his own weight with family and household matters so she, in effect, has a third child. Mary feels abandoned by Bill's denial of responsibility for the family and the energy he puts into friends and work. Mary resents Bill's attitude so much that she can barely contain her anger in front of the children.

Bill views his work and household chores as his contribution to the family, while Mary's work is played down as an interim measure to support their current lifestyle. He is angered by what he sees as Mary's attempts to control him. He can't stand her nagging and withdraws. He wonders whether he was really ready to have children. Bill finds himself bored at home since the birth of their first child when all of Mary's energy went into the children. He was disappointed that he no longer was "number 1" in his wife's affection, so he put energy into life outside the family. He was angry about that.

Mary grew up in a household where her mother stayed home and took care of the family. Mary was the oldest of six children. Her mother seemed always to be angry and exhausted, requiring Mary to pitch-in to help with the younger children. It just never seemed to be Mary's "turn." Her mother never had time to participate in Open School Night activities or attend her violin recitals in grade school or debates in high school. Though her father was a work-a-holic and was often unavailable, she knew that she was his favorite. She treasured the memory of his attending a PTA meeting at which she played her violin in an ensemble. She often defended him when her mother's anger at his absences led to strife and recriminations.

Bill grew up as the only child of a dairy farmer and his unhappy pianist wife. Bill's parents had little time for him. His mother harbored dreams of reviving her musical career and spent much of her time giving piano lessons and practicing. His father was an emotionally remote man who busied himself with the farm and working on his antique automobile. Bill did his chores and watched his father tinker, but his father's remoteness made Bill feel invisible. Bill complained that they never went anywhere. His father cited the daily need to care for the cows to justify their difficulty leaving the farm. Bill was bored at home and was forced at an early age to look for entertainment elsewhere. He spent afternoons after school in the homes of friends when growing up. He was popular at school and was elected president of his high school class.

Mary and Bill grew up in families in which their parents were little disposed to meeting their emotional needs. If their parents had been so disposed, Mary and Bill probably would not be recreating for their children similar difficulties in coping with the stress of life. Neither received from their parents the necessities of emotional needs – the support that comes from unconditional positive regard, the structure of appropriate <u>limits</u> to guide their development, or the stimulation of relevant <u>challenges</u> to heighten their capacities.

Positive self-esteem is the result of dealing with the varied demands of our lives. To do this we are required to face our fears. We may fear not knowing how to deal with certain challenges because they will show us up as inadequate, for example. When this occurs in an atmosphere of clear and appropriate limits along with sufficient but not too much support and challenge, we have the confidence to face and deal with daily events. By so doing, we learn about ourselves from these experiences and develop emotionally. On the other hand, we may avoid these learning opportunities because limits are too unbending or too loose, support is too meager or overindulgent, or challenge is overwhelming or insufficient. The outcome is blocked or distorted emotional development.

We clarify our emotional needs as our lives progress. To the extent that these needs are met – we feel safe; we have a variety of experiences; and we feel valued for ourselves. Thus, we develop emotionally with positive views of ourselves. To the extent we do not have these needs met, our emotional development is thwarted and distorted. We develop a hidden and negative view of ourselves.

Emotional development usually begins in some sort of family. Families vary from one another and within (for example, birth order) in the extent, ways, and times they provide appropriate conditions for their children. Consequently, there is a great deal of variety in the extent to which families provide the necessary ingredients for emotional development. The following formulation of six emotional needs is based on the ideas of Virginia Satir.[9]

APPRECIATING INDIVIDUAL DIFFERENCES

When there is acceptance and appreciation, we feel respected and unique. As the result of positive and appropriate responses to our varied actions, we gain a sense of belonging and feel "special." This treatment is the foundation for developing a separate identity. When acceptance is lacking, we feel tolerated at best and unknown at worst. This results in a sense of alienation and uncertainty about who we are and where we belong. Our beliefs about ourselves are negative (for example, "If you really knew me you wouldn't like me.")

In order to gain some security in an uncertain world, we may manipulate others and the environment as well as shape ourselves to avoid negative reactions from others. Alienation and uncertainty about one's identity can have a variety of serious negative impacts. More familiar for our purposes is the morbid concern with what others think and the obsession with performing roles to find a place for oneself. Feelings of rejection and abandonment generate self-rejection. Unable to act assertively, we are aggressive or submissive. Thus, we forfeit the deeply meaningful adult connections so necessary for a sense of belonging.

---

[9] *The New People Making.* Mountain view, CA: Science and Behavior Books, 1988.

LOVE, TENDERNESS, AND CARING OUTWARDLY EXPRESSED

When there is love, caring, and tenderness expressed, we feel safe and nurtured. Reaching out for support and attention and receiving non-possessive affection and emotional intimacy in return permits us to feel lovable and comfortable with vulnerability. To the extent that the outward expression of affection is lacking, we feel unlovable, unsafe, and needy. Attention getting may substitute for caring in a child's attempt to gain nurture and support. Touching and intimacies may feel invasive to those trying to cope with an ever-present sense of rejection. When adults abuse them, children may retreat to a position of "not being there" to defend themselves.

Adults who feel unsafe and needy have difficulty trusting others, yet they may make dependent connections. Their fears of neediness and unlovability generate self-rejection along with a deep yearning for love. We may have difficulty caring for and pleasing ourselves. Unable to say "no" to enmeshment with and manipulation by others we may permit abuse. We may be more concerned with taking care of others than being responsible for our own safety. Or, self-protection may requite us to say "no" to any request for meaningful contact. Unable to risk vulnerability, we forfeit emotional intimacy.

MISTAKES AND ERRORS ARE OPPORTUNITIES TO LEARN

When adults encourage exploration and experimentation, children approach learning, challenge, confusion, and creativity with minimal stress. They gain a sense of mastering challenges from experimenting and seeing mistakes. Errors are considered a basis for learning. When mistakes and errors are viewed as features of inadequacy and worthlessness, children fear challenges, become uncertain about their ability to respond effectively, or receive encouragement to look outside of themselves for answers. Despite the value given to accomplishment and certainty, achieving our goals does not raise our self-esteem more than momentarily.

Adults who feel inferior and inadequate often have difficulty trusting their abilities. They nervously question the "rightness" of answers and worry interminably about making mistakes. Confusion is intolerable. Beliefs emphasize unworthiness or stupidity. Fear of being wrong generates desire for perfection. The difficulty involved in saying "yes" to challenges precludes self-reliance and forfeits emotional development. Saying "yes" to challenges, for the purpose of looking good or to prove something, often leads to despair and the belief that one is an impostor in the face of achievement.

RULES CLEAR AND APPROPRIATELY FLEXIBLE

When rules are clear and appropriately flexible, we feel supported because we know our boundaries will be respected. A sense of stability and purpose results from our action within a clear set of rules. Some flexibility in rules teaches us respect for human needs over an impersonal order. Absent, ambiguous, and/or inflexible rules may teach us to fear abuse. We may become anxious about vague limits and/or alienated by inflexible limits. To the extent that children are anxious and/or alienated, they may become rule-bound, rebellious, distant, or erratic. Children will see their family as chaotic and lose hope of experiencing stability.

Adults who have difficulty saying "no" are unclear about boundaries – where do they stop and others begin? They easily become enmeshed in relationships, either "losing themselves" or isolating themselves. The fear of rejection makes it hard to hear or say no. Without a sense of boundaries we feel helpless to resist abuse and manipulation by others and believe we are inadequate. Adults who are rigid about rules have their fear of disorder close at hand. They may be negatively judgmental about different or creative activities, preferring to view the world in absolute, right or wrong categories. The fear of confusion is based on the anxiety that without certainty the world will fall apart, while they miss finding their humanness in flexibility. They are very demanding of themselves and others.

RESPONSIBILITY MODELED

When our elders take responsibility for the consequences of their actions, we learn self-reliance, the value of the freedom to choose, and to act with care and compassion. "Can do" expectations by our caretakers develop within us a sense of ownership for our actions. When we see responsibility avoided or honored in words but not in deeds, we develop a sense of helplessness about our ability to influence events; we become cynical about the hypocrisy observed; and/or we are arrogant about the effects of our actions on others. Teen-agers often believe that

41

there is something "wrong" with them because they are "different" in some way. This belief may encourage a socially approved irresponsibility, which emphasizes surface features – following fads, manipulating others, avoiding blame, and testing the limits.

Adults who have learned to shift responsibility to others or distance themselves from the results of their acts make it difficult for themselves to learn from their experience. Fearful that others may blame them, they may be quick to blame others in a vain hope to avoid responsibility, only to see their efforts fail and accomplishment elude them. Insensitivity to feedback about their actions avoids facing their fear of their own powerlessness and reduces the likelihood of learning from their experience.

HONESTY IN COMMUNICATION AND TRUST IN RELATIONSHIPS

When communication is honest we learn to be open and direct in our speech, sensitive to the credibility of others, appropriately spontaneous and trusting in our relationships, and appreciative of our feelings and those of others. When communication is dishonest, secretive, or guarded, we learn to withhold, to be devious in our speech, suspicious or credulous of others, restrained and untrusting in our relationships, and fearful of our feelings. Being closed and mistrusting others, we block our spontaneity and attempt to control our world behind a wall of isolation and fear. Teen-agers may try to manage the world they perceive to be spinning out of control by stonewalling adults or manipulating them. Distrusting ourselves we fear risking our brittle sense of self in a rejecting world.

Fear of rejection makes it difficult to reach out for support from others, thus maintaining a self-fulfilling prophecy of isolation. Playing roles protects our vulnerability while we appear to be extraverted.

> As a child I used to think about my father and mother, "These people don't know that I'm a person, too, that I'm not a toy they happened to make.
> – V.S. Naipaul[10]

[10] V.S. Naipaul (2001). *Half a Life*. NY: Knopf

> Within you there is a stillness and
> sanctuary to which you can retreat
> at anytime and be yourself.
> – Hermann Hesse

Chapter 5

THE IMPORTANCE OF FEELINGS

Judy and Jim are in their early forties. They are quite successful in their careers and have no children. Often they are at work late, partly as a way to avoid spending time together. Judy and Jim were high school sweethearts and married after their sophomore year in college. They thought they would have children, but when it appeared they could not their relationship changed. They still involve themselves in community and church activities as a couple, but otherwise they spend increasing amounts of time at home separated from one another. They both come from families that stayed together "for the children" and in which there was a great deal of conflict. Their fear of conflict is so great they made a pre-marital promise never to argue. They are still married twenty years later, but they do not talk about anything that matters. They are very angry at each other but suppress it to honor their agreement. Their private thoughts are focused on fantasies of travel, adventure, and sexuality. On the evenings they are home together they can be seen at their separate computers surfing the Internet.

Judy and Jim are suffering. They maintain the illusion that if they do not own their feelings, the feelings do not exist. Their avoidance of angry feelings prevents them from knowing themselves and developing the skills they need to deal with the conflict they fear. Their lack of self-knowledge leads them to fear trusting themselves to be OK without each other. Their anger covers up this fear. Their sham relationship avoids conflict by denial and isolation. Their expression is skewed. Their energy is directed into fantasy and compulsive habits.

Feelings are the gateway to our inner life by informing us about our needs. They are our involuntary internal reactions to external situations and serve as our early warning system about life events, good, bad, and in between. Feelings contain information from our perceptions of life situations and the meanings we make of them. The greater the variety of feelings we sense, the more information we gain, the more options we perceive, and the more varied actions we can take. Thus, feelings are the basis of choice about our actions. Gendlin said it best when he made the connection between feelings and understanding.

> When what I feel unfolds, when I explicate it, when it comes to me what it is I feel, then it always turns out to be all about my situations, what people did to me, what it means I must now do, why I can't do it, what I'm up against in trying, and so on . . . . [F]eelings are how we are

in a situation and this is especially noticeable when we are confused, troubled, stopped, or upset. We feel the situation, but not clearly, not in a way we can lay out in actions we will take, or in words we can say. Therefore anyone interested in how we live in our situations must be interested also in our feelings, especially when these trouble us, and are unclear.[11]

Many of us misunderstand the role of feelings. Having the wrong idea about feelings blocks us from using knowledge derived from our feelings to guide our actions. Many of us grew up in families that had rules suppressing feelings as dangerous, wrong, and bad. We learned to "stuff" our feelings or be criticized or ridiculed. We were told "don't cry," but we heard "don't feel." By so doing, our caretakers sanctioned separating our feelings from our actions and thoughts. Stuffing feelings led to our believing that the pain associated with these feelings was not tolerable.

When we impulsively respond to circumstances, we do not acknowledge our feelings, so we miss out on the information they contain. This allows external circumstances or other individuals to define situations for us. Thus, we are forced to rely on external cues, the needs of others, or events to guide our actions. One effect is to give up our power, opening the door to being manipulated, exploited, or abused.

A second effect of impulsive action is we fail to base our actions on internal criteria. We are led to self-defeating or self-destructive action that we regret and

[11] Gendlin, E. (1968). Psychotherapy and Community Psychology. *Psychotherapy: Theory, Research and Practice, 5*: 68.

which usually confirms our sense of unworthiness. These consequences are devastating for emotional growth and self-knowledge. When we do not have access to our feelings, we do not learn to distinguish between feelings and actions. For example, some see violence as the equivalent of anger rather than as one (rarely appropriate) among many expressions of anger. Similarly, many of us find it difficult to say "I am angry," without raising our voice.

There is also confusion about the origin of feelings. We justify the inability to acknowledge our feelings by saying, "He (or she) *made me* feel." No one can *make* us feel anything. We make ourselves feel what we feel. The common sense notion about catharsis illustrates this confusion. Some people confuse impulsive rage reactions with catharsis. It is used to justify the yelling and hitting associated with anger of frustration. Catharsis may purge negative feelings, but, if it does so, it is only for a short time. Such a catharsis can also increase anger by all parties in the situation. In any event, the next time the situation occurs, which produced the feelings in the first place, will produce them again. The most unfortunate consequence of this notion about catharsis, however, is that it usually targets helpless persons vulnerable to adult aggressors.

Automatic violent and emotionally abusive actions sever the connections among intertwined thoughts, feelings, and actions. When we abuse others, we are so self-absorbed we have no idea that our rage hurts anyone. Awareness of our effect on others is cut off. Afterward, when our rage declines, we may become aware our behavior was an over reaction. We may rationalize saying, "I couldn't help it," or "I was just expressing myself," or blame the victim of the abuse for causing it. Being responsible for our abusive action and using this knowledge to motivate change rarely occurs.

Associating feelings with pain is common. This can make access to feelings distressing and often blocks them. The pain we feel connects with childhood experiences in which we were unable to escape or change the abusive or neglectful situations and about which we were unable to talk. Since we have survived and grown however, we now have abilities and access to resources we did not have then. We need to understand that the pain can never be as bad as it was then. There may be discomfort, but we can survive.

Some families only permit the expression of those "sunny" and positive emotions pertaining to happiness and joy. Children learn that there are "right" and "wrong" ways of feeling and they are only "OK" when they appear happy. There is little guidance for what to do with the darker side of their experience – their anger, sadness, and fear. Children learn to suppress these feelings, but given their inevitability, they may be converted into shame, violence, depression, or anxiety. When we feel angry, afraid, or sad we may think we are "bad."

By being open to our feelings we connect ourselves to our needs and wants in the immediate moment. In this way, feelings access our self-knowledge and help us adapt to situations about which we may not have enough information. Feelings retrieve information, which may not be in our conscious awareness. This helps us to organize our actions for problem solving.

Feelings replace facts when we do not have other information to help us understand a situation. For example:

> ***Anger*** is our emotional reaction to a perceived <u>violation</u> by an abuser of our rights or boundaries. Anger mobilizes our energy for self-protection, to protect our loved ones, to stand our ground, to say, "no" and to fight for our rights.

> ***Fear*** is our emotional reaction to a perceived <u>threat</u> of immediate danger. Fear mobilizes our energy to avoid, to withdraw, or to flee.

> ***Sadness*** is our emotional reaction to a perceived <u>loss</u>. Sadness mobilizes our energy to repair the loss or mourn the end of a relationship.

> ***Joy*** is our emotional reaction to a perceived <u>validation</u> coming from an achievement or the demonstration of support. Joy mobilizes energy to affirm the event.

The renowned psychologist Carl Rogers once explained that the more words we have to describe our feelings, the greater control we have over our emotional expression. If, for example, the only word we have for anger is rage, the only way we can express anger is through violence. We become "like a bull in a china shop." If we had words like "irritation" or "annoyance," it is more likely, according to Rogers, that we will express our anger in a less violent way.

Almost anyone can learn to think or believe or know, but not a single human being can be taught to feel. Why? Because whenever you think or you believe or you know, you are a lot of other people: but the moment you feel, you are nobody-but-yourself.
– e. e. cummings

PART II

> ## We've met the enemy, and it is us.

CHANGE

The basis for pessimism about personal change emerges from experience and research showing that people who fail to maintain lifestyle changes predominate. Studies of stopping smoking, weight loss, exercise, cardiac rehabilitation, and substance abuse recovery programs indicate that 75 to 80 per cent of participants relapsed a year after their "change."[12] Thus, change making has the well-deserved reputation of being difficult and painful. Yet, it is also compelling and possible, since 20 to 25 per cent maintained the change. Success in changing turns out to be a struggle, which requires skill, tenacity, and perspective on the part of the change maker.

Some of the fear of making these lifestyle changes comes from a concern that a change will make us "someone different." This prospect of the loss of self, which may not be consciously recognized, can block the willingness to risk – so necessary for any change.

[12] Gross, S.J. (1994). The Process of Change: Variations on a Theme by Virginia Satir. *Journal of Humanistic Psychology, 34* (3): 87-110.

The truth is that no matter how hard we try, nothing is ever lost. Some events or habits may recede in memory or importance, but they can never have *not* happened. This is why, much as we might want to, we cannot just eliminate the ways of thinking and acting associated with low self-esteem. In fact, we raise self-esteem by facing and reconstructing these old ways of thinking and acting. What has changed is that the old ways no longer fit our current life situation. We drop the old ways in favor of ways that do fit. This is why when we raise self-esteem, we transform ourselves into "being more of ourselves."

This section reflects my understanding of the process of change. For many years I have been guided by eminent psychologist Kurt Lewin's theory that change occurs following the decrease of resistance to change rather than the increase of the pressure to change. I have learned to be deeply respectful of resistance as a reasonable, if mistaken, expression of people's sense of who they are. This has led me to take into account and include in this section two rarely considered preconditions for change – hope and safety.

> Whether you think you can or
> think you can't, you are right.
> – Henry Ford

Chapter 6

UNDERSTANDING CHANGE

Thirty-five years ago, I was a pack-a-day smoker. My nine year-old son, fearful of what he was hearing about the effects of smoking on the TV, began nagging me to stop. After a month of his nagging, I began to hear him. Perhaps, he was right. Not only was it a serious health concern for me, but second-hand smoke was putting my family at risk. Shortly afterward, I had the idea of placing myself on a smoking diet. I set up the diet regime to include not smoking for an hour after meals and no more than one cigarette an hour. During the next three months, there would be times when the hour was only twenty minutes long, but I persisted with the diet despite these lapses. Just as I was beginning to gain a sense that I could stop smoking, I succumbed to the flu. After three days of illness, when smoking was intolerable, I awoke on the fourth day feeling better. With some prodding, I was able to decide not to light a cigarette at that moment. I felt the familiar craving to smoke for several days but was able to resist it. Finally, after several more days, I found my desire to smoke evaporate, reappearing only in some social situations. Though I weathered the worst of the cravings and never smoked again, cigarettes were in my dreams for another year.

This is a true story of the beginning of a number of my life-changing events. In this case, I established a long-range goal, which I whittled down to several short-term objectives. The long-range goal developed, because I listened to my son, and it was something I really wanted to do anyway. I made my son's feedback personally meaningful. Then, I did not rush things but gave myself some time to work out a plan. After doing so, I was able to accept the lapses that occurred periodically without succumbing to the guilt over them that can turn a lapse into a relapse. I persisted on this path for some time until something unexpected happened – *I became aware that I was in control of the smoking*. This, then, permitted me to take advantage of having succumbed to the flu for three days. Had I not worked to increase my self-control, the advent of three days of not smoking would probably not have been sufficient to enable me to keep my vow. The plan I used was crucial to my success. The vignette also reveals the power of resistance. Though when I was awake I had no conscious desire to smoke, the habit involving a familiar object, took a while to clear my dreams.

Raising self-esteem begins with self-caring changes in lifestyle (See Part III). To begin with, this includes stopping substance abuse and other unhealthy habits. Afterward, self-caring activities such as exercise, eating healthfully, maintaining appropriate weight, and lowering stress demonstrate our belief in self. Making such deliberate, intentional changes can be difficult to achieve. Some people make lifestyle changes as a result of their own efforts. Others do so in conjunction with therapists and self-help groups. Change frustrates many others.

WHAT MAKES CHANGE SO HARD?

Real change can be difficult. Our resistance to it preserves our sense of "who we are." We are not just obstructive. As we grow, we develop a lifestyle that stabilizes the events in our lives; interprets the meaning of these events; and disposes us to seek consistency. The emotional bonds of our relationships cement these events into our way of life. Our attachment to this lifestyle is so strong that it has us resisting change even when the advantage of change is obvious.

Change involves the unfamiliar and stimulates confusion, the true enemy of change. Change involves the loss of something we value, thus involving sadness. Change can stimulate concern about our competence to manage it, prompt our fear of failure, and raise a question about our self-worth. With all these potential outcomes, it is no wonder that ambivalence about change is common. So, it turns out that though we may yearn for change, we may fear it at the same time.

Our beliefs are potent sources of resistance. Miriam Nelson and her colleagues[13] classify five categories of beliefs that help us maintain the status quo. These include:

> Emotional (depression, guilt, fear, and sadness): "There's too much stress in my life to change."

[13] Nelson, M. E., Baker, K.R., and Roubenoff, R. (2002). *Strong Women and Men Beat Arthritis*. NY: G. P. Putnam's Sons.

Environmental (physical arrangements associated with making the change): "I have no where to go to exercise."

Physical (pain or disturbance accompanying change): "I am too tired to exercise."

Social (where our action is influenced by others): "My family is against my making these changes."

Cognitive (our interpretations of situations): "I can't find the time."

TRIGGERS FOR CHANGE

Change is not always difficult. It depends on whether we are talking about basic or "cosmetic" change. A cosmetic change is in appearance only. These changes usually do not threaten us. We may consider some changes affirming, like getting a suntan. We incorporate such surface changes into our lifestyle without altering the basic pattern of our lives. Deeper changes require a strong influence to trigger a change, for example in addictive patterns. Someone who stops smoking but begins snacking compulsively, for example, has not changed his or her addictive lifestyle.

The difficulty involved in change is related to how threatening it is to our sense of self. The loss of the familiar or fear of the effect (cravings) stimulates resistance. The more the change threatens us, the stronger our resistance to it. When resistance is strong, our reason to change must also be strong, if we are to make and maintain change. Usually we resist by ignoring, discounting, or rejecting the necessity. We might deny the problem, for example, by saying, "I can give up alcohol any time."

However, if we are persistently aware of the motive for change, we may become quite uncomfortable and confused by our ambivalence. This ambivalence is about our wanting to stay the same on one hand versus our awareness of our need to change on the other. The resulting confusion triggers physical arousal. It, then, may take something like physical pain to push us to make the connection between our fear of loss (if we do change) and our fear of not surviving a health problem (if we do not). The process, however, plays itself out differently for each person. A "black out" may stimulate one person to stop drinking but not another.

Other events that carry with them a strong motive for change are new experiences, personal loss, and social pressure or social support from a close relative or spouse. Special events can shift us from one role to another. This might include a work promotion, marriage, or parenthood. Some events can also rearrange our lives, for example, the onset of menopause, a child's school commencement, or the loss of a job.

DISCOMFORT AND CHANGE

The eruption of the tension to both resist and move toward change propels us into a state of flux that we experience as confusion and discomfort. A sudden disarrangement of what we previously assumed about ourselves combines with the disappearance of predictability. In a moment the familiar becomes strange. We fear the loss of security, become angry about an imposed change, or feel sad over the loss of an imagined future. The discomfort poses questions: Will we grow by facing our feelings and develop needed coping skills or deteriorate through escape into defensiveness? Negativity occurs when we see the trigger event as a threat. We experience danger in the discomfort. The following possibilities heighten the danger:

- Loss of control;
- Lack of familiarity with the trigger event or few skills or resources to respond to it;
- Lack of trust in ourselves to handle the threat;
- Limited access to people with the expertise to deal with such troubling situations; or
- Distance from emotional support.

The perception of danger leads to the physical arousal we experience as discomfort. Though discomfort can signal danger, change need not be profoundly disturbing. We can prepare ourselves for change by restoring a sense of hope about our possibilities and finding a place of safety to pursue them. In this regard it is helpful to know:

- Discomfort is a normal part of the process. Some fear is natural when confronting the unfamiliar as is sadness in the loss of the familiar. By acknowledging the fear and sadness we diminish thinking we are "abnormal."

- The fear that making changes evokes in us as adults could never be as bad as the terror we felt as children. We have a lot more experience, skill, and resources available to us now than we had then. We have a voice now. We did not have one then. We know more now than we did then. We can do more now than we could then. There is more help from others now than was available then.

Making Change

Though we require strong motives to change intentionally, it is a mistake to translate "strong motives" to mean "greater intensify of effort." This interpretation is often the basis for failure in change making, as we soon tire of putting all that effort into the process. It can also encourage denial of responsibility. We may believe we have to wait for others to change before we do or that we need to make others change. If we want change to occur, it is essential that we make it entirely our responsibility.

Planning for Change

We can make some changes happen. We can follow a formal planning process to anticipate and reduce the risks of taking action. Stop smoking plans, for example, are more likely to be effective when smokers taper off their use and intermittently have short periods where they do not smoke before they finally quit. Joining twelve-step groups gives many alcoholics the support to stop drinking. We can also act "as if" we have made the change. This way we can get feedback about the change without making a final commitment. Many change goals respond to taking carefully selected steps. We incorporate the step into our lifestyle and allow it to settle before moving on to the next step. For example, to reduce fat intake, change just one dish at a time. One way to start making changes is with options for which you have a strong motive, that fit your lifestyle, and which you can share with others.

When the goal is more global (for example, self-esteem) and the plan less clearly formed, change appears to require letting go of the attempt to exert control over the process. This might mean examining, for example, what we might lose in making the change. When unacknowledged, the potential for this loss could surface as resistance to the change. It is also important to release ourselves from the expectation that we must micro-manage the process. Instead, by adopting an active and experimenting attitude, we can become free to learn about ourselves and the process of change. The following strategies are examples.

- **Reduce resistance** – Since real change is linked with a sense of danger, reducing the threat may make it less disturbing. One way of doing this is to view the change from a new perspective. We can reframe it as a puzzle, for example. This redefines change as a dilemma, instead of danger, allowing excitement to replace the discomfort. Approaching the dilemma as a detective would provides energy for the change, much like adrenalin does for hang-gliding or a single-minded focus does for playing a computer game. Discovering how smoking has affected our lungs might make stopping smoking a "learning-how-to" challenge. Another approach is to reorder priorities, for example, via a "write your own epitaph" values clarification activity. With change reframed in this way, risk and fear can be reduced.

- **Shift the context** – Often we are embedded in roles and other social arrangements, which dictate how we approach the change process.

For example, many of us are familiar with the helplessness assigned to the victim role. Learning to think like a survivor instead can help us to develop a more assertive approach. Victims tend to focus on the negative, the half empty glass, what can't be done. Survivors focus on the positive, the half full glass, what we *can* do. Just beginning to look for something to do about our situation stimulates hope and further action. This can place our fear on the "back burner."

- **Change expectations** – What we believe can become a self-fulfilling prophecy. Challenging these beliefs and looking for alternative expectations can change the outcomes of our actions. The negative triggers we bring to making changes may involve not making a mistake or being "perfect" in some way. These unrealistic expectations prevent us from taking the risks central to making changes. We may become stuck in making changes because our expectations are too high. Awareness of the power of our beliefs can help us to consider what is really important to us and make our expectations more reasonable.

- **Self-awareness** – Self-awareness is crucial to making many of the changes needed to raise self-esteem. This approach to change focuses on finding ways to block the energy that powers the habit we want to change. This means we shut off what supports the habit much like the electrician shuts off the electricity when he works on our house wiring. Habits continue because we lack awareness of the impulse that drives them. Despite their self-defeating or self-destructive outcomes, they go unchecked because the feedback (for example, bodily feelings) that would otherwise come with the experience is blocked. Directing our awareness to the habit can unblock the feedback. This gives us choices about coping with stressful situations. It is no accident that one feature of successful weight-loss regimes is keeping a daily diary of everything ingested.

Though real change in habitual patterns is a continuing struggle, research[14] shows that most people making intentional change attempt multiple times before a change is consolidated. This means several things. We need to think about change efforts as learning opportunities, rather than "life or death" efforts. We need to consider what we can learn from the effort and how to make a positive response when we fail. Failure can be helpful!

Planning is essential. It can include a careful assessment of anticipated problems, lowering those risks, and identifying alternative actions. It might also include how to prepare beforehand and what practice would help to facilitate change. Beyond that, when the going gets tough, we need to avoid beating up on ourselves when we do not meet our expectations. *This is a puzzle to solve. It is not a new way to judge us.* Put pressure to succeed on the shelf. Trying harder usually does not work. Lowering risks does. Be gentle. Break the change down into smaller pieces. Take one step at a time. Make it good.

[14] Gross, *Op. cit.*

The "Bottom Line"

When we behave impulsively we reveal a potential agenda for change. At some point our impulsive overreaction is sufficiently self-defeating or self-destructive to give us a reason to change. This is referred to as one's "bottom line." The following vignettes show how some people find their bottom line, while others never do.

> *Ferdinand was had been smoking marijuana for over ten years. He found it calmed him, and he had no reason to think it affected his life in any way. That is, until, as the result of a drug screen, he lost his job. Since he had free time, he went to see a drug counselor.*

> *Helen was a sixty-year old alcoholic who was sent to our clinic by the local district court as part of her sentence for driving impaired without a license. She did not object to the referral and seemed glad to have someone to talk to. She also made it clear, however, that she had no intention of ceasing drinking. This took on a special significance when she shared her diagnosis of liver cancer.*

> *Angel was a seventy-year old smoker with emphysema who was well known in her neighborhood. She was a sight to see smoking while she dragged the oxygen cart she needed to help her breathe.*

> *Henry, now fifty-five years old, had been married to Martha for thirty-five years. Together they had six grown children. He was*

a chronic binge drinker who would make his family miserable with his ranting and negativity when he drank. When he wasn't drinking, he was a quiet and non-threatening. After his last binge, Martha had finally "had it" with him. With all the children out of the house now, she was the only target for his drunken rage. She went to an alcoholism counselor who suggested an "intervention." This is a safe way for family members to confront the substance abuser. Henry was reluctant to go to the intervention but consented when he understood the alternative was to leave the house. Being so self-absorbed, he was astonished to hear Martha and the children tell him how his actions had hurt them over the years. They also shared their concern that he was drinking himself to death. He agreed to go to an alcoholic rehabilitation hospital.

Stages and Levels of Change

Though change in self-esteem is complicated, we can simplify it. Earlier we presented the five levels of self-esteem. Following the first level of low self-esteem, the second level involves ending addictions and dependencies. Doing this prepares us to move ahead to the third level, as we no longer bury our fears in substances and rituals. Here, we work at maintaining self-care. Such action is rewarding in itself. Here, we tell ourselves we are worth the effort and that we are capable of taking care of ourselves. This, subsequently, aids us at the fourth level to dispel confusion and the arousal that accompanies personalizing negative events and our coping impulses. The fifth level focuses on the transformation process.

As we move through these levels, knowledge about the change process helps us to know on what to focus. This means that at any one of these levels, we could be at any one of seven stages in making a change. Each of the following stages[15] (See Diagram # 3) represents a different change problem, thus it may call for a different type of action.

1. **Unaware of need to change** – We deny any need to make a change in our lifestyle. We reject, discount, or are unaware of Information, physical pain, or events that can trigger awareness of the need to change.

2. **Acknowledge need to change** – Acknowledgment begins with awareness that we need to make a change, but we are vague about goals or are not ready to consider taking action. Then, naming the need for change, perhaps by acknowledging the personal consequences of not changing, we can trigger its acceptance.

3. **Accept need to change** – We know we have to make a change and are more specific about goals but have not actually planned how to change. Thinking about a strategy can trigger preparations to change.

4. **Prepare to change** – We consider how to take action and are developing a plan to do so. Reducing the risks of change can trigger action.

[15] Based on Prochaska, J.O., Norcross, J.C., & DiClemente, C.C. (1994). *Changing for Good.* NY: Avon Books.

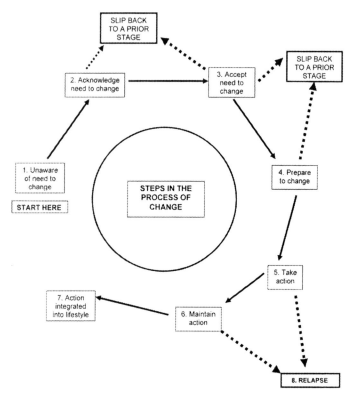

Diagram # 3 – Visualizing Stages of Change

5. Take action – We act on a plan, which replaces a prior action with a new action. The new action is directed at a specific goal that can be described and measured.

6. Maintain the action – We have been performing the new action for a period of time. Our commitment to the action may be made uncertain by cravings to return to old behavior. Relapse prevention activity can help to maintain change.

7. Action integrated in lifestyle – Our commitment to the action is at the point where we are beyond cravings and lapses. This change process is completed.

8. Relapse – Relapse means we have tried out a new action but have returned to a previous action for, at least, a semi-permanent period. The personal consequences of not changing can trigger a return to the new action.

There are many ways to go about making change. My experience leads me to caution that we can find the task of making changes overwhelming, especially when we see all the options available. The confusion here can lead us to conclude that raising self-esteem is impossible. Nothing could be further from the truth. As I have said, it is hard at times. There is no magic. What does work is "hanging in there" and figuring out what has been effective in the past. Examine our past experience in making changes. What worked? What did not work? How do we need to reduce the risks of change? Reviewing our past, considering the array of self-care options, and identifying situations that may prove difficult all will assist making a successful plan for change.

MAINTAINING CHANGE

A fact, borne out by research, is that many people who make intentional changes fail in a short period of time. For three-quarters of successful change-makers, the change is a distant memory by the time a year has passed. Many fail to appreciate the power of resistance to change. Others do not know they need to take a different approach to maintaining the change than it took to making the change in the first place. These failures give many change efforts a revolving door character. Maintaining change requires we prepare for the very real possibility of relapse and deal again with old stresses. Here is how relapses occur and what we can do about them:

Relapse Path	Corrective Actions
Sometime after actually making a change, the demands of maintaining it seem to outweigh whatever advantage we received for the new behavior.	*We forget that resistance is a normal part of the process of change. Reaching out to talk with a supportive person at this point could clarify our thinking.*
We are disappointed by these events.	*We forget that let downs are part of living.*
We feel deprived, victimized, resentful, and blame ourselves.	*Note "red flags." Talking with a supportive person would help to clarify the situation.*

Then it occurs to us that our old behavior (smoking, isolation, inactivity) would help us to feel better.	*We forget that our old behaviors made us feel worse. Talk to someone, exercise, or self-soothing would help relieve pressure.*
Cravings for the old behavior begin, undermining our desire to continue to care for ourselves in the new way.	*Cravings are a "red flag" for potential lapse. If we do not have a plan, we need one to divert our attention.*
The smell of a cigarette attracts us, another group member annoys us, or we overdo the exercise.	*More "red flags!" Acknowledge the difficulty of making a change. Talk to a supportive person or distract yourself.*
We say, "I told you so. This new stuff will never work." Cravings increase.	*This indicates we need to employ an option to divert our attention.*
We risk exposure to old ways – enter a smoke-filled bar, mingle with cynics, or see a friend who hates exercises.	*These are "dangerous situations" that put us on a slippery slope toward relapse. Put diversion plan into effect.*
We ignore the "slippery slope" focused as we are on the old behavior.	*Now is the time to put our plan into action or we increase the risk of a lapse.*

The cravings keep increasing.	*"Red flags" are waving. Our poor coping skills, no alternative plan, and refusal to reach out, increase the risk of a lapse.*
When we begin to think the old behavior will reduce the cravings, a lapse in maintaining the new behavior is likely to occur. We smoke a cigarette, avoid support group meeting, or miss our regular exercise appointment.	*The lapse is a result of our resistance to change. We can go back to steps we took prior to the lapse, guilt-free. At this point a supportive person could clarify the situation. The cravings will not go away until we cope with them while sustaining new behavior. A program of new ways of thinking and acting, psychotherapy, self-help groups, diet, and exercise could contain and reduce cravings.*
Guilt and no plan lead to relapse.	*Try again.*

Examine the Nature of our Commitment to Change

Many decisions to change eventually fail because the original commitment was to relieving symptoms, pleasing others, or denying the strength of our resistance to change. We are more likely to maintain commitment to change if it focuses on a change in lifestyle, not just changing a habit. In effect, we commit to staying with the new behavior from the moment of change into the foreseeable future.

Clarify the Difference between a "Lapse" and a "Relapse":

If a lapse occurs it is important to understand that lapses are normal occurrences in change making. The lapse is the result of failing to make or effectively implement a plan to deal with our ambivalence and/or disappointment about the change we have initiated. Returning immediately to the new behavior will render the lapse a mere slip. If the lapse produces guilt, it is likely to turn into a relapse into old pre-change behavior.

Recognize the Possibility of Relapse:

As the pleasure and/or support involved in making the change declines, (and it will) be prepared for ambivalence and/or disappointment. Expect that the old pre-change behavior will appear attractive again. Remind yourself why you made the change in the first place. The desire for magic may obscure the benefits of making the change at this time.

Identify Typical "Red Flags" and "Dangerous Situations:"

Craving for the old pre-change behavior, impulsive action, and agitation may surface as well as "finding" ourselves in situations dangerous to our new behavior.

Prepare a Plan for Dealing with Cravings:

Make a plan for how to divert our attention. Include likely "dangerous" situations and associates that invite old behavior.

Our plan needs to include clear objectives, risk management, alternative activities, use of coping skills, and access to support resources, such as twelve-step groups. Rehearsal of relaxation, stress management, and assertion skills can also be helpful.

When Cravings Increase, Initiate the Plan:

Rehearse coping skills including, relaxation, stress management, and assertion skills.
If we start thinking that the old pre-change behavior will reduce the cravings, a lapse is likely. The only hope of permanently reducing the cravings is to maintain the new behavior. Cravings eventually subside with a continuing effort to maintain new behavior.

I will act as if what I do makes a difference.
– William James

Chapter 7

FOSTERING HOPE

I was amazed at the impact of my decision to stop smoking on my beliefs about myself. Lurking in the background of my thinking was the belief that I could not give up smoking. Once I believed that I could give up smoking, it all seemed easier, somehow. Though I had achieved some of my lifetime goals, first as a student and later as a professional educator, I realized that whenever I come close to anything new I had approached it with great caution. I connected this awareness with my usual first impression that I feared I was incompetent. I learned in high school that I had to address that fear and act differently to get anything done. I grew up thinking I could not do things on my own – that without others helping me I was helpless and hopeless. The expectation that I "couldn't" followed me into adulthood. It did not always stop me, but it did interfere with my approach to action and decision-making.

My breakthrough on my smoking issue was based on my transition from hopeless to hopeful. "Can't do" implies hopelessness, while "can do" implies hope. Hope sets up an expectation that success is possible, making it more likely. Though hope is a powerful motive for change, it is not easy to get there. We need to understand what makes us so hopeless in the face of change.

So, before there is change, there is hope for change. Hope taps into our yearnings to alter our lives, to realize our dreams, end our despair, assure our luck, achieve our desires, validate our ambitions, or confirm our trust. Hope does not include wishful thinking, greedy obsessions, lust, gullibility, blind faith, false promises, or ignorance of unwanted side effects. These attitudes disregard realities, overlook pain and sacrifice, or block flexibility.

One way to build hope is to tell ourselves that we have more resources for change than we think we have. To begin with we may not believe it, despite its truth. Repetition makes a connection with our inner selves that our conscious mind does not fathom. Start off your day and your change efforts saying this true statement aloud:

> **The fear that change evokes now could never be as bad as the terror I experienced as a child. I have a lot more experience, skill, and resources available to me now than I had then. I have a voice now. I did not have one then. I know more now than I did then. I can do more now than I could then. There is more help from others now than was available then. There is hope for me.**

DEFINING HOPE

- **Hope is a positive forecast**, an opening to the future. Hope is the oil that greases the skids of change. It poses the possibility that we can improve on our lives. Hope is an attitude that imagines a possible future, affecting our judgments about uncertain situations, so that we anticipate movement in a positive direction.

- **Hope is a prophecy for success**. Positive expectations tend to be self-fulfilling, because they produce action in the direction of realizing the forecast. Hope stimulates us to bring energy and commitment to situations that, in turn, tend to tip the scales in the direction we want them to go. It also offers us a head start by suggesting concrete pathways and options for change.

- **Hope springs internal.** Our personal needs, values, and beliefs engender hope. Hope stimulates our motives and supplies the energy for change

WHAT NURTURES HOPE?

Action is the handmaiden of hope. Just as hope can lead to action, action can lead to hope. Realizing hope requires that we move from thinking and observing to acting. Nurturing hope is a way of reducing the risks involved, so that anxiety does not impede action. Though becoming more hopeful is easier said than done, people have been able to raise their dim hopes in the following ways.

- **Clear goals energize hope**. A goal is a purpose, motive, or reason for the use of time or for the justification of an activity. The simplest way to foster hope is to examine the goals that emerge from our desires and ambitions. The more these goals are:

☐ Concrete (rather than vague),
☐ Achievable (rather than lofty),
☐ Challenging (rather than easy), and
☐ Appealing (rather than dreary),

the more likely we are to believe that acting on them will make a difference in our lives. The test of a useful goal is its ability to motivate constructive action.

Developing goals begins with asking, "What do I want?" Goals may also emerge from value clarification exercises, imagining our "possible selves," considering our self-care needs, or identifying the tasks that emerge from our attempts to meet these needs.

- **Accept losses and limits**. Action to change something usually involves the loss of something valued. A geographical move may require changed relationships with loved ones. A change of jobs may require the loss of a skill, an opportunity, a future, or a dream. Loss often leads to our feeling sad and angry. Our willingness to talk honestly about the loss and to own the anger and grief, represents the first steps in mourning the loss. By grieving, we acknowledge the loss as something "that happened;" we open ourselves to learning something from the experience and how to get on with our lives; and we turn our despair into new goals congruent with a new reality.

- **Examine resources**. The knowledge, skills, and strengths we bring to our endeavors generate hope. It is instructive to look back at our past successes and challenges overcome to rediscover the skills, tactics, and hope that generated past accomplishment. Reaching out to others to gain their insight, perspective, experience, advice, and support is an important way of extending the resources available to us.

- **Think "can do."** The children's story "The little engine that could" is an example of creating hope via our belief in self-empowering action. Seeing ourselves as the "actor in the piece" is reassuring and affirms taking further action. The following techniques kindle hope:

  ☐ **Concentrate on small steps** – According to an old Chinese saying, "The longest journey begins with a single step." Consider a single step in the direction you seek. If the step is the right one, you will progress. If not, you have learned something and you can try another approach.

  ☐ **Prioritize steps** – Review possible steps, and choose those that fit your best guess about what will promote progress or convey information about appropriate tactics.

  ☐ **Rehearse action** – Some actions require practice beforehand to clarify and firm up your approach. Role playing or practicing a presentation before a mirror or with an audio or TV tape recorder can offer valued feedback.

  ☐ **Tolerate errors** – For many, the hardest lesson of all is to learn that we progress when we take action, regardless of whether we succeed or fail. It has been said, "The worst thing that can happen is we might learn something."

☐ **Normalize barriers** – Achieving one's goals is often difficult, especially when these goals are challenging and meaningful. Accept barriers as part of the process and plan around them.

☐ **Act "as if"** – When unsure about a goal, pretend a commitment to it thereby giving yourself an "out" before you begin. By acting with this "out" in mind, you gain information without obligating yourself to stay with it. You can always say, "I changed my mind."

☐ **Reduce risks** – Anticipating hazards and needed resources can reduce the risks of taking action. Becoming clear about the risks involved, the potential for losses, people and other resources available, what can go wrong, and how you will know – these are all helpful in deciding whether the risk is worth taking. Some risks are dangerous while others are over-inflated, so it is important to be able to distinguish among them. Taking the time to pursue your goals in the way you desire permits a sense of ownership of the effort. Allowing for shifts in goals and strategies, a fail-safe point and a back-up position, and tolerating failure as a learning experience are all attitudes that give us the flexibility to tolerate risk. Ironically, acknowledging the anxiety that so often attends risk can help to calm us.

Chapter 8

MAKING IT SAFE

Many people back away from making changes because it feels dangerous. In this chapter we clarify the nature of this threat and describe some ways of reducing the sense of danger. The following true statement helps us to focus on what needs to be done. Though, on first reading we may not really believe it, repetition makes a connection with our inner selves our conscious mind does not fathom.

> **I want to be responsible for providing for my own safety when I make changes. I believe I need others to keep me safe, as I do not know how to do it myself. It scares me to think about what I must do. At the same time, I know the more I rely on others to make life and change safe for me, the less safe I really feel. Though I tend to feel hopeless and helpless, the only hope for me is to help myself by trying to figure out how to provide my own safety.**

THE PATH FROM DANGER TO SAFETY

The usual reaction to uncertainty is confusion. Many of us associate confusion with the expectation of harm, thus it is frightening. Fear, in turn, elicits a natural self-protective impulse to safeguard our life and health. This readies our bodies for action. A narrowing of attention filters out information not relevant to the threat, while increased activity prepares us for action. This state of vigilance, begun by confusion, prepares us to deal with an emergency – to fight or flee. Our ancient hunter/ gatherer forebears survived encounters with hungry carnivorous animals or hostile humans because they were able to act in an emergency. Concentration on the threat at these times may become so intense that thought processes become rigid and emotions are either blocked or overwhelming. These reactions pre-empt what normally competes for our attention and result in a sense of mental and emotional disorganization.

In this way, fear temporarily erases such adult skills as maintaining boundaries and taking assertive action. Our panic erases our willingness to reach out to support resources we know are available. Facing fears requires these skills and resources. It is crucial to growth to become aware of our fear and choose to face the confusion. We need to create a place of safety to face the confusion. With a sense of personal safety, we can take the day-to-day risks necessary to face our fears, learn from our experience, and make the changes we desire. We need to consider how to make a friend of confusion.

Creating safety is an ongoing task. As we learn how to gain and apply the coping skills and access the support resources needed, we can defuse threatening situations. We do this by first considering our safety plan to be a work in progress. Then, we grow gradually in our capacity to feel in control and safe by creating zones of empowerment. This means bringing our skills, resources, and beliefs to bear in threatening situations and learn how to defuse their threat. Each time we do so, we acquire an additional zone of empowerment. We can create zones of empowerment as the consequence of:

- Learning to feel in control of ourselves in a threatening situation;
- Developing the skills needed in the threatening situation;
- Finding a basis of trust in ourselves to handle threats;
- Connecting with mentors and models who have the expertise to deal with such troubling circumstances; and
- Involvement with people from whom we can gain emotional support.

SUPPORT RESOURCES

Emotional support comes from relationships in which we feel we belong; in which we perceive that someone cares about us; and which have continuity. These relationships reduce the anxiety associated with change. If we do not have such relationships, we can find them in self-help groups and reach out to people who have had similar experiences.

- **Groups** – Groups involve us with like-minded individuals, giving us a sense of belonging and validation. Many find a comfortable beginning in self-help groups where there are people who have had similar experiences.

- **Individuals** – Notice the people you know who are models for behavior and attitudes that, by example, can take you beyond the narrow confines of your own experience. By doing so, they legitimate those alternate ways of looking at and dealing with things that previously you had not considered or feared to consider. <u>Mentors</u> are those special individuals whom we look to for their relevant experience and who are somewhat further down the path in life on which we would like to go. Mentors share their information and advice in a relationship, which helps us to make opportunity and avoid pitfalls.

COPING SKILLS

Coping skills include various attitudes and actions. We can deal with fear by reducing its customary response – physical arousal. Learning to tolerate this discomfort includes: using relaxation skills to "slow down" and devising risk reduction activities. We can employ problem solving techniques to calm and emotionally distance ourselves. This may involve "can do" attitudes about considering options and following-through in effective and self-caring ways. (More on coping skills can be found in Chapter 12.) Here is an example of my use of coping skills to adapt to a changing situation.

Finally, I had to face it. The hills in my hometown and my suffering knees were putting an end to my twenty-year long-distance running career. Knowing I required aerobic exercise, I decided to try swimming. I was not a strong swimmer, so I began slowly. I swam one or two lengths of the pool at a time, but I found it boring. I noticed I felt uneasy in the deep water. I also discovered to my surprise that I felt especially alert and positive after swimming, much like I had after a long-distance run. I decided to find a way to swim longer distances without stopping and to make it all more interesting. I asked and received help from the lifeguards with my swimming stroke. One day while swimming in the deep end of the pool I remembered my fear of water harkened back to when I was two years old. I was happily playing at the water's edge when I was suddenly swamped by a huge ocean wave. Remembering that event eased my anxiety. I turned counting out the number of lengths I was swimming into a mantra for meditation. I soon lengthened my distance to eight, then sixteen, and finally twenty-four pool lengths without stopping. This gave me the aerobic effect I wanted.

I coped with my problem with a concrete objective, by asking for help when I needed it; by using my self-knowledge to allay my fear; and by adapting a meditation technique.

AUTOBIOGRAPHY IN FIVE SHORT CHAPTERS

By Portia Nelson [16]

I. I walk down the street.
   There's a deep hole in the sidewalk.
   I fall in.
   I am lost. . . .I am helpless,
      It isn't my fault.
   It takes forever to find a way out.

II. I walk down the same street.
    There is a deep hole in the sidewalk.
    I pretend I don't see it.
    I fall in again.
    I can't believe I am in the same place,
       But it isn't my fault.
    It still takes a long time to get out.

III. I walk down the same street.
     There is a deep hole in the sidewalk.
     I see it is there.
     I still fall in….it's a habit.
        My eyes are open.
        I know where I am.
     It is my fault.
     I get out immediately.

IV. I walk down the same street.
    There is a deep hole in the sidewalk.
       I walk around it.

V. I walk down a different street.

[16] Reprinted with permission. Copyright © 1993 by Portia Nelson, from the book THERE'S A HOLE IN MY SIDEWALK, Beyond Words Publishing, Inc., Hillsboro, Oregon, USA

PART III

What should I do?

SELF-CARE AND SELF-ESTEEM

Now we begin to detail how to raise self-esteem. Our purpose here is to capture, by our own efforts, a sense of comfort, safety, hope, and inner control. These will allow us choices in life that lead to increasing our self-esteem. As I outlined in the Introduction, the work we do here progresses in a stepwise fashion. Specific goals are discussed in a progressive order – goals at the lower levels must be achieved before higher-level goals can be usefully approached. To move up from level ❶ low self-esteem means coupling disciplined plans with realistic objectives to achieve goals at four higher levels:

> ❷ Contain addiction,
> ❸ Improve self-care,
> ❹ Slow personalizing, and
> ❺ Grieve the loss of childhood.

"Self-care," which includes Levels ❷ and ❸, is discussed in Part III. "Slowing personalizing," which includes Level ❹ and "grieving the loss of childhood," which includes Level, ❺ are discussed in Part IV and V.

85

The material in this section does not do full justice to the struggles many people will face as they work on making suggested changes. At the same time, it is clear that any sustained containment of addictions and habituations are goals that have been achieved by many people. It depends, according to Dr. Robert J. Petrella,[17] on three general factors: insight into the nature of the addiction, the degree of commitment to recovery, and what positive steps the person is willing to take. Though we offer some insight into the first two factors, this section is devoted to identifying the positive steps to negotiate the path to containment and to identify the issues encountered along the way. Before proceeding please note the following:

- Each level in the path toward sustained containment calls for a major commitment of energy, action, and openness to feelings. Moving through the following two levels may take an extended period of time and provide continuing tests of commitment. Our problems in living did not develop overnight. We may not solve them in a day, a month, or even a year. The experience of many people supports the idea that cravings for old behavior eventually subside with persistence.

- Many people find it confusing to read about a level more than one level above their own skill development. As we solve the tasks of each of the lower levels, our understanding of the higher levels increases.

[17] Petrella, R.J. Understanding Baker's Alcoholism. *The Boston Globe,* January 10, 2004, p. A121.

TWO LEVELS OF SELF-CARE

Growth beyond Level ❶ low self-esteem begins with the first two levels of self-care.

LEVEL ❷ has to do with dependence on substances and compulsive activities called habituations. Habituations include codependency, sexual and relationship "addictions," spending compulsions, binge eating, gambling, controlling others, and raging. If any of these apply to you, containing them is a priority. These dependencies are similar to substance addictions in that they block the fears we must face to raise our self-esteem. They also nullify the positive effect of other self-care options. Doing without your substance or habit will increase your cravings for them in the short term. Learning to deal effectively with these cravings will result in a reduction of shame and a more positive self-esteem. It will also permit you to work effectively at the next level of incorporating other self-caring practices into your life.

LEVEL ❸ Introduces you to self-affirming actions, which, when maintained, result in reducing cravings. You will also begin feeling better about yourself. As these self-caring activities are maintained, you become ready to move to Level ❹, reducing the personalizing of stressful events. By that time, yo*u will believe you deserve it.*

Progress will be slow, at first. With diligence you will see one or more of these changes.

- Awareness of the connection between negative events and impulses: Because you won't "have to" act out every time you become confused, you will see a decrease in impulsive responses to negative events.

- <u>Less overwhelming arousal</u>: As you become more aware of your feelings, they will become less explosive. You will become aware of how your fear has interfered with your effectiveness and self-care.

- <u>Increased choice about how to act in stressful circumstances</u> rather than as you have previously in "either/or" extremes.

- <u>Awareness of difficulty in saying "no"</u>: The boundary between "I" and "you" will be clearer, thereby reducing abuse by others.

- <u>Understand that you really cannot control other people</u> to "make" them give you what you want. Your best shot is to ask for what you want, while accepting they need not comply.

- <u>Decrease in everything being about you</u>: You will see yourself more as a survivor and less as a victim. This will allow you to stop blaming yourself for negative events. Instead, you will see that you and others share a contribution to them.

> The point is not to do remarkable things, but to do ordinary things with the conviction of their immense importance.
> – Teilhard de Chardin

People say, what is the sense of our small effort? They cannot see that we must lay one brick at a time, take one step at a time. A pebble cast into a pond causes ripples that spread in all directions. Each one of our thoughts, words and deeds is like that. No one has a right to sit down and feel hopeless. There's too much work to do.
– Dorothy Day

Chapter 9

CONTAIN ADDICTION AND HABITUATION

The discovery of self begins with owning our addictions and habituations. These destructive habits provide a highly structured way to avoid experiencing our feelings. Ignoring our feelings means that we do not learn about ourselves from our life encounters. Avoidance also means we fail to practice self-care, which is essential if we are to act on a positive belief about ourselves. Instead, we look outside ourselves to a substance or activity for a clarity we do not know how to provide for ourselves.

> *Peter has been drinking heavily for years. He began as a teen-ager. He had a lot of fun "partying" when he was younger, but now, after a night of drinking, he often wakes up feeling lousy and with little memory of it. He disregards his resolutions to limit his drinking when in a bar. Old buddies with whom he drank in years past no longer frequent his hangouts.*

Stanley J.Gross, Ed. D.

> *They are either dead, in jail, married, or in AA. He does not really think he has a drinking problem. He tells himself that he has stopped before and can again. It is just that his work as a carpenter foreman on a dangerous job makes his life so stressful.*

> *Peter drove home drunk from his favorite bar once too often. Stopped by a policeman who had noticed his impaired driving, he tested drunk on his sobriety test. Later, while he was waiting in court for his case to be called, he had the sudden thought that it was his drinking that spun his life out of control. Previously he thought it was his work. Maybe it was the other way around?*

Peter is on the edge of discovering the elaborate game he plays with himself. He attempts to maintain an impression of control over his inner experience of stress. Yet, he becomes dependent on the very activity used to control it. The result is, paradoxically, he loses control over the process.

ADDICTION AND HABITUATION

Substance Abuse

Physical dependence upon alcohol or drugs involves:

- Requiring the substance to reduce withdrawal cravings;
- Inability to control when and how the substance is used;
- Requiring an increasing amount of the substance to become intoxicated; and

- Spending an increasing amount of time seeking out the substance.

Signs of addiction include hangovers, blackouts, poor health, tremors, mood swings, alienation from family and friends, and involvement with law enforcement. Depending on the level of dependency, some alcoholics and drug addicts require detoxification. *Detoxification from alcohol and drugs may require medical supervision!*

When the dependence is on an activity or a ritual, it is called a "habituation." Habituations may include: codependency, sexual and relationship "addictions," spending compulsions, binge eating, gambling, and raging. Though usually not quite as directly dangerous or physically debilitating as substance dependence, these rituals are incorporated into our lifestyle and may be as difficult to change.

Other Addictions and Habituations

Smoking addiction – Smoking is an alternate addiction for many working on sobriety. Smoking increases the risk of heart disease, breathing and circulatory problems while decreasing physical capacity, energy level, and sensory awareness. Millions of people have found a way to stop smoking, even though it is quite difficult. Nicotine is considered the most addicting drug when compared to other drugs. Most smokers find stopping smoking to be accompanied by strong withdrawal symptoms. Success requires strong desire and a disciplined personal plan. Self-help, treatment, and informational programs (for example, Lung Association) are widely available.

Eating "addiction" – A narrow focus on *compulsive dieting* for the sake of beauty can be habituating. Ignored in the insatiable quest for the "perfect body" is the fact that formal weight control programs are notoriously unsuccessful in the long run. Most people who rely on weight control programs wind up a year later at their original weight or heavier. This so-called "yo-yo" effect of the weight loss/gain cycle is very stressful on the body. Recent research suggests that excessive dieting may raise, rather than lower, the "set point" of our natural weight level. This makes it harder to lose weight in each subsequent weight loss effort. Sensible weight reduction requires lifestyle changes in how and what we eat and incorporating exercise into our daily activity. Some suggestions are:

- Alter living spaces to discourage overeating;
- Eliminate purchases of snack and highly processed foods;
- Avoid "fast food" restaurants;
- Keep a food diary to identify problem eating habits;
- Calculate calories in food and beverage intake;
- Develop realistic expectations of what you can accomplish;
- Calculate calories burned during physical exercise; and
- Practice relapse prevention.

Weight control is less difficult when we exercise, have good social support, address our problems directly, and have reasonable weight control goals (for example, avoiding further weight gain or eating a healthy diet). Paradoxically, focusing directly on weight loss sabotages weight control efforts.

Emotional factors can be predictors of weight gain. This suggests that learning alternate ways of dealing with depression, anxiety, anger, and worry is a key element of weight control.

Binge eating involves the compulsive intake of an excessive amount of food well beyond the point of satiation. Bingeing on snack foods, candy, and fast foods or eating large amounts of food on festive occasions often occurs when we are under the influence of negative emotional states.

Bulimia and *anorexia nervosa* take compulsive dieting and bingeing to a more self-destructive level. *Bulimia* usually involves an excessive concern with body shape or weight, episodes of binge eating, and the regular use of purging, fasting, or excessive exercise to prevent weight gain. Heart and kidney problems, menstrual irregularities, electrolyte imbalances, gastritis, glandular enlargement, and erosion of dental enamel are some of its medical complications.

Anorexia nervosa involves an intense fear of being fat, a distorted body image, and a body weight 15 per cent or more below normal. Medical complications include death, heart and kidney problems, estrogen deficiency, low blood pressure, anemia, elevated cholesterol, muscle weakness, and osteoporosis. **The severity of the physical consequences of bulimia and anorexia nervosa requires early medical intervention!**

Sexual "addiction" – Sexual "addiction" is an alternate addiction for many working on sobriety. Preoccupation with sexuality in one's lifestyle may suggest that it serves a habituating purpose. In this case, sexual behavior is non-relational with lustful, not loving characteristics. Sexually "addictive" behavior might include, among others, combining obsessive use of pornography with compulsive masturbation, frequent promiscuous sexual activity, or recurring extramarital affairs. As is the case with other addictions and habituations, excessive sexual activity relieves anxiety, depression, and loneliness; involves loss of control; and creates harmful consequences. Cessation stimulates withdrawal symptoms.

Codependency – Codependency is a widespread habituation. It shows itself in couple and family relationships. Mutual reliance is a desirable aspect of intimacy, but codependency actually blocks intimacy. Ignoring our own needs in favor of the needs of others, masks fear and is not an expression of love. By trying to gain support, validity, protection, and/or control we can actually lose ourselves. In codependency, our lack of knowledge about our own needs has us acting in some of the following ways:

- When we lack clarity about our boundaries (knowing where we end and others begin), we may permit abuse and refrain from self-care;
- By giving our power away (by pleasing others, not ourselves), we may feel helpless;
- By looking to others to know what we need and how to act, we reveal that it is too important to us what they think;
- If we believe that others will meet our needs if we meet theirs, we become resentful when they do not;
- When we need others to make us feel whole, we may stay in failed relationships;

- If we expect that others will see the world as we do, we may not understand that they have wants and needs which are different from ours; and
- By hearing only information about ourselves, we become self-absorbed.

Codependency is a feature of many couple and family relationships. When our close relations do not live up to our codependent expectations, our negative beliefs about ourselves are verified. We think we are wrong, bad, inadequate, and to blame for whatever negative happened. Since this is hard to accept, we deny the blame (avoid the fear) by placating, manipulating, or resenting these close relations. At the same time, we are willing to do anything to avoid rejection by them. So we may enable them in their addictions by tolerating inappropriate behavior to "keep the peace."

When we avoid our fears in this controlling and self-absorbed way, we distort our perception of events and circumstances to be entirely "about us." We have difficulty detaching from or having empathy for others. Enmeshed with others, we judge ourselves by their behavior toward us. Our over-concern about what others think about us has us projecting our anxieties onto them so that what we see is a reflection of our needs. What we fear others will say about us is what we actually think about ourselves!

A CONTAINMENT PROGRAM

Ending the use of substances, rituals, or activities may be easier said than done. To improve our self-esteem, it is essential we end our dependence on them. These addictions or habituations have helped us avoid the emotional pain resulting from life's stressful events. Thus, we have lost those opportunities to face our fears. Failing to use these opportunities to learn about ourselves, our self-esteem has become stunted.

The following options offer help to contain these addictions and habituations. These options can assist us in acknowledging our dependency on them, accept them as previously necessary but no longer fit, and find a way to give them up. This will take some time and much effort. Diligently following the options below, all of which contribute to the goal of containment, will end self-abuse.

The Goal

Contain the addictions and habituations spawned by coping impulses. Recognize that sobriety is essential to any further growth.

The Immediate Problem

There is a natural ambivalence when making any change. In particular, giving up addicting substances and habituating activities involves the loss of what has been familiar. It may raise questions about self-worth. Doubts about one's ability to change are common. Any of these reactions can shake one's determination and may create strong cravings.

Tasks

Addictions and habituations are formidable! Ending dependency on substances and activities increases craving for them, but persistent containment can reduce them. Addictions and habituations become less overwhelming with programs that include self-care, reaching out for emotional support, and accessing needed resources.

Many of us find it difficult to face our fears, our self-absorption, and our cravings. Change in the direction of containment often waits for the pain of a life out-of-control, physical or mental illness, shattered relationships, families in disarray, bankruptcy, violence, or jail. The point at which we are not willing to tolerate further pain is our "bottom line."

> *She knew she was overweight, and she knew the situation was quickly reaching the point where it was beginning to affect her health, not to mention her self-image. She knew, as well, that she needed to gain control of the situation. So, every morning before work, she resolved to do something about it. "Today, I'll control my eating. I'll get a good start on my diet," she told herself. "In fact, I won't eat anything for breakfast and just have a little something for lunch. The less I eat, the more weight I'll lose and the faster I'll lose it." And that is just what she'd do – skip breakfast and have a cookie or two or maybe a diet drink for lunch. But something was wrong. She wasn't losing weight; in fact some weeks she was gaining. But then she thought about it, and she realized what was going on. By the time she got home from work, she was so hungry she began eating and really didn't stop for the rest of the evening. She had rationalized her behavior by telling herself that, although she did enjoy a good dinner every night, her other eating was only "piecing." But the more she thought about*

> *her "piecing," it added up to a heck of a lot of food – and a heap of guilt. "And you know," she told herself, "despite all that food, I'm never really satisfied nor am I enjoying eating." It was then she decided to seek help.*[18]

The subject of this vignette demonstrates a flirtation with the bottom line familiar to people who are substance and activity dependent. Her rationalizations allowed her to continue to ignore her binge eating. She finally became aware she was eating a "heck of a lot of food," she had loads of guilt, and she felt unsatisfied. These factors combined to define her bottom line and drive her to seek help.

Get and stay sober. Strictly containing our dependence on a substance or an activity is essential. Sobriety or containment requires than we recognize our reliance on chemicals or rituals as a form of self-abuse. In the past, this reliance has been very effective in eliminating emotional pain from the stressful events in our lives. As a result, we have not learned from our life experience, nor developed the skills needed to face life's challenges. Instead, we have blocked our emotional development. Change requires we acknowledge our addictions and habituations, accept them as previously necessary but no longer fitting, and find a way to give them up.

Reach out. Ending dependency is hard to maintain alone, because it arouses cravings. We can expect increased confusion when we try. Avoid isolation by reaching out:

---

[18] Hayhurst, S. (2002). Food for Thought. *Indiana State University Magazine, 5* (3): 30-31.

- <u>Communicate</u> with supportive and accepting people,
- <u>Access</u> your own support network,
- <u>Join</u> support groups, and/or
- <u>Contact</u> professional clinics.

Support groups have people just like us to offer information and a different perspective to deal with our confusion and craving. Support groups include recovery groups for many kinds of addiction and dependency: Alcoholics Anonymous, Narcotics Anonymous, Al-Anon, Codependents Anonymous, Adult Children of Alcoholics, Debtors Anonymous, Gamblers Anonymous, Sex and Love Addicts Anonymous, Overeaters Anonymous, and Smart Recovery. These groups:

- Provide social support to combat isolation;
- Create a positive identity to replace the legacy of shame;
- Puncture addictive pride and self-deceiving pretensions;
- Provide a language where one did not exist to discuss what had not been discussible;
- Offer a cognitive context for self-care; and
- Promote a model of self-governance to replace unhealthy behavior.

Professional clinics have trained therapists offering groups, classes, and personal counseling.

Admit our role in the problem. Acknowledge our addiction and loss of control. How does this loss contribute to our distress? What is its impact on our lives?

Exchange the victim role for a survivor's role. Recognize that we *are not* responsible for what made us an addict, but we *are* responsible for what we do about it now. A survivor looks at *how* to find a way to let go of shame and make the attitude shifts to move on.

Develop a plan. Practice self-care, reach out to others, and access necessary resources. This approach helps us to limit cravings and restore hope. With addiction, we tend not to practice self-care. Diminished or absent self-care skills, vague boundaries, and limited access to feelings all allow self-abuse. An active focus on a healthy lifestyle is an alternative to addiction. A plan includes:

- Self-care activities, including exercise, relaxation, sufficient sleep, and a good diet;
- Continuing support for containment;
- Relapse prevention – identifying "red flags" and avoiding dangerous situations; and
- Acquiring assertion skills (See Chapter 15).

Use information as an aid to growth. Most substance and activity dependents miss out on learning things our non-addicted peers learned at an earlier age. Even in information-rich situations, such as AA meetings, we may fail to listen or discount crucial information. Reading, listening, and learning about sobriety and the nature of addiction and dependency can help us feel less helpless and more normal. A trip to the local bookstore will reap dividends.

Write about the experience. Put pen to paper to describe the ingredients of the plan and our experience with it. This not only provides a needed release for our pain, it helps us to feel more in control of what is happening and puts self-care in the forefront of our thoughts.

Prevent relapse. After achieving containment, a second plan is necessary to maintain it. Craving for the old behavior is the major problem at this point. Coping with cravings is aided by two assumptions of relapse prevention. First, there is an important difference between "lapse" and "relapse" – a lapse is a one-time event. Second, continued coping with cravings while maintaining new behavior will eventually reduce the craving. The following options may be included in a plan that brings together diversion activities, coping skills, and emotional support:

- Use arousal reduction procedures when feeling cravings (slowing down, distraction, self-care, self-soothing);
- Recognize negative emotions as "red flags" (indicators a lapse may follow if you try to ignore them);
- Avoid "dangerous situations" (associated with places, people, and events of known risk of eliciting old behavior);
- Make friends with non-addicted persons;
- Develop new activities (not associated with addiction and dependency activities);
- Find effective ways to deal with pressure and negative emotional states (distraction, self-care, self-soothing, reaching out for help, stress management);

- <u>Rehearse</u> responses to predictably difficult circumstances.

The process of recovery from addiction and habituation is ongoing. In the vignette below, John's recovery had progressed so well he felt ready to marry and have children. When there was stress on the marriage and his wife had little understanding of recovery from alcoholism, problems arose. Here, John preserved his recovery program and responded to his wife's needs at the same time

> *John has been married to Susan for almost four years. He got sober about two years before meeting her. Susan recently gave birth to twin girls. After the help from family and friends faded away, they found themselves at loggerheads over how to deal with Susan's need for help in the evenings and John's need to attend AA meetings.*

> *John had no objection to helping. He took care of the twins on the weekends (together with Susan) or alone when she left the house to run errands or to visit family and friends. His problem was that attending AA regularly was the bedrock of his sobriety program. He believed that if he did not keep up with his meetings, he could begin drinking again, a situation that would be disastrous for both he and for his family. After discussing this problem with his sponsor, John agreed to brown bag his lunch and attend noontime AA meetings near his workplace three days a week. This freed up three evenings to help Susan and preserved his regular AA attendance.*

Alcoholism is a strange animal. Sometimes I can watch people drink and it doesn't bother me. Then I'll see a beer commercial and break into a sweat. I'll see an ad in a magazine for a wine I used to enjoy, and the craving is so intense I'll become nauseated. It's an awful struggle.
– Lee from *The Chamber* by John Grisham.

Chapter 10

IMPROVE SELF-CARE

> If I am not for myself, who will be for me? If
> I am only for myself, what am I? And if not
> now, when?
> – *Hillel*

Self-care options include a variety of life style habits
and ways of thinking. The following options can
relieve stress in the short run and raise self-esteem
if practiced diligently. However, some people will find
the sheer number of them overwhelming. Keep in
mind that we incorporate these skills and attitudes
over time. So, arrange for your first steps to have
some obvious benefit, but at the smallest cost. Other
important self-care practices are mentioned here
only in passing: getting regular medical and dental
examinations; avoiding risky and life-threatening
activities; practicing safe sex; and maintaining a safe
physical environment.

Because this chapter is about adopting specific
actions, we begin with the following outline.

The Goal – *Develop a self-caring lifestyle.*

Prerequisite – Success in containing addictions and
habituations.

Immediate Problems – Making changes in substance
abusing actions and destructive habits is quite similar.

In both cases, choosing containment produces ambivalence. Also stress, unfamiliar challenges, and unaccustomed opportunities arouse forgotten feelings. The resulting confusion is unsettling, prompting strong desires to return to our old behavior. Consequently, many people experience several lapses before making a continuing commitment.

Tasks – Rely on group support, self-care, distraction, and other new activities. Eight techniques are discussed in this chapter. Our program now directs us to concentrate on these tasks to support the emergence of our inner strength.

- *Self-soothing* – By diverting the physical and emotional arousal that attends stress, we create a sense of calm and safety.

- *Exercise* – Exercise for increased capacity, strength, and flexibility raises cardio-vascular capacity, reduces stress and depression, and burns excess calories for weight control. Recent research shows minimal exercise is better than none.

- *Maintain a healthy diet* – A wide variety of unprocessed, low-fat foods provides the nutrients for healthy living and reduces the risks of physical illness, stress, and mood changes.

- *Maintain a healthy weight* – Combining exercise and diet options allow us to approach our ideal body weight.

- **Relaxation** – Relaxation techniques have an immediate and long-range impact on stress and the quality of life.

- **Maintain healthy sleep** – Getting eight hours of sleep a night increases alertness, receptivity, and concentration.

- **Maintain sexual health** – Sexual activity, which is an expression of loving rather than lusting, heightens our joy in life experience.

- **Maintain spiritual health** – Connection with something larger that ourselves gives purpose to our lives and support to our on going experience.

SELF-SOOTHING

Self-soothing safely reduces the physical and emotional arousal that occurs when we are stressed by negative events. These options work partly because they distract us from the event and partly because they have a direct affect on how our body functions.

Attend to breathing: When we are stressed, our breathing is usually flat, short, and labored. In this case, our breath goes into our upper chests or shoulders. This type of shallow breathing into our upper torso increases the stress on our bodies. On the other hand, breathing slowly and deeply into our abdomen relieves stress. Sometimes called "belly" breathing, it calms us by influencing the autonomic branch of the nervous system. The technique appears simple. The stomach pushes out as the breath goes in.

This is the way babies breathe and how we ourselves breathe when asleep!

Grounding helps us detach from emotional reactions to upsetting events. By shifting our focus away from the event, grounding helps us to gain control of our arousal. We ground ourselves by paying attention to some neutral aspect of our physical environment, such as picture the shape, size, and color of nearby objects or focus on the smells and the sounds perceived.

Attend to posture: Crooked, stiff, or off-balance describes the body under stress. When sitting, our legs may be stiff and both legs and arms may be crossed in a defensive posture. When standing, we may lock our knees. Our body is tense. Instead, we uncross our legs and arms, sit or stand up straight using our backbone to support our bodies, and place feet firmly on the floor. These postural shifts support balance and strength and distract us from the stress-inducing event.

Cultivate mindfulness: This centering technique focuses our attention on what is happening to us in the immediate moment, rather than attending to other people, the past, or the future. We close our eyes and pay attention to our breathing and our body. Becoming gently aware of what we see, hear, or feel in a deliberate way will, after a few moments, slow our reaction. We can also focus on our physical sensations and breathing while taking a walk or sitting quietly by ourselves.

EXERCISE

"If you do just one thing, make it exercise." This is the title of the first of a series of articles on self-care.[19] There is good reason for this statement. Exercise improves fitness, strength, and flexibility. As it does, we increase our capacity to handle negative events and improve our appreciation of ourselves. Taking care of ourselves is an alternative to cravings and self-abuse. It provides a focus for our effective use of time and for stress reduction.

Capacity –Vigorous exercise (heart racing and body sweating) for 20 to 60 minutes a day, three to six days a week increases endurance and stamina by improving cardiovascular capacity. Other benefits include releasing endorphins (which have a role in reducing stress and depression) and burning excess calories, leading to weight reduction. Brisk walking, jogging, cycling, aerobic dancing, swimming, stair climbing, and cross country skiing qualify as vigorous and restorative exercises, if done properly. (*Be sure to clear such an exercise program with a physician if you have not been exercising or are 40 years of age or older.*)

Recent research shows that even a minimal level of exercise is better than none. A regular routine totaling 20 to 30 minutes a day, three to six days a week will improve fitness. Choosing a type of exercise we really want to do will help us incorporate it into our lifestyle. Even then, it may take three months or more of practice before it becomes routine. Activities, such

---

[19] Tori DeAngelis (2002). If you do just one thing, make it exercise. *Monitor on psychology, 33* (7) 49-51.

as walking at lunchtime, dancing, gardening, tossing a ball, and climbing stairs, can provide a sufficient amount of exercise to maintain body tone and alertness. The 1996 Surgeon General's Report made the recommendations in Diagram # 4 for exercise at various levels of intensity. Powers[20] suggests three indicators of intensity level – Low (we are able to sing and exercise); moderate (we can talk while exercising); and strenuous (we have trouble talking).

Even exercise can be too much of a good thing. Excessive exercise may indicate that we are exchanging one addiction for another. When we exercise despite significant pain or give it a priority beyond good health and normal social, family, and work relationships, it may be serving another purpose. Too much exercise can lead to recurrent overuse injuries, excessive weight loss, depressed immune system, and arthritic and degenerative changes.

Strength training maintains the mobility, flexibility and power of the body's muscles, tendons, ligaments, and joints. It increases metabolism, which acts to keep weight and blood pressure in check. Estimates are that if we do not do strength training we will lose 35% of lean muscle mass and 20% of strength by the time we reach the age of 65. This loss of strength has a progressive impact. It affects the ability to do everyday things, such as walking up stairs, carrying groceries, getting up or down from chairs or the floor, and maintaining balance. Strength training using all the major muscle groups is recommended at least twice

[20] Powers, M. (2003). *Eating Right When You Have Diabetes.* Hoboken, NJ: John Wiley & Sons.

More vigorous, less time	Medium vigor & time	Less vigorous, more time
Stair walking 15 minutes	Swimming laps 20 minutes	Walking 1 ¾ miles 35 minutes
Shoveling snow 15 minutes	Water Aerobics 30 minutes	Wheel wheelchair 30-40 minutes
Running 1 ½ miles 15 minutes	Walking 2 miles 30 minutes	Gardening 30-45 minutes
Jumping rope 15 minutes	Raking leaves 30 minutes	Touch football 30-45 minutes
Bicycling 4 miles 15 minutes	Pushing stroller 1½ miles, 30 minutes	Volleyball 45 minutes
Playing basketball 15-20 minutes	Fast social dancing 30 minutes	Washing windows or floors, 45-60 minutes
Wheelchair basketball 20 minutes	Bicycling 5 miles 30 minutes	Washing/waxing car 45-60 minutes
	Shooting baskets 30 minutes	

Diagram # 4 –
Examples of Moderate Physical
Exercise[21]

[21] *Physical Activity and Health: A Report of the Surgeon General.* (1996). Atlanta: National Center for Chronic Disease Prevention and Health Promotion. Retrieved March 14, 2000 from the World Wide Web: http://www.cdc.gov/nccdphp/sgr/sgr.htm

a week. One indirect result of strength training is the ability to increase food intake without gaining weight because of muscle development. Marian Nelson's *Strong Women Live Longer* [22] (suitable for men too) describes a scientifically based, user-friendly program of weight training.

Flexibility is moving one's joints through a maximum range of motion without pain. The need for flexibility increases with age, especially if we are over 50 years of age, because of disuse of muscles. Disuse affects the ability to reach, carry, grasp, and balance. By building flexibility, we improve daily functioning and avoid unnecessary injury, pain, and surgery. Stretching exercises involving all muscle groups three times a week are recommended. Leg stretches after aerobic activities maintain flexibility and minimize pain and injury following exercise. As a general rule, stretches need to be held from a gentle pull to a point just prior to discomfort. We need to do this for thirty seconds and for two repetitions. Stretching needs to be done following a five-minute warm-up activity to avoid injury and after all aerobic and strength training. For more about exercise see Kate Hays' *Move Your Body Tone Your Mind* [23] and a guide that is not just for older people.[24]

MAINTAIN A HEALTHY DIET

The U.S. Department of Agriculture recommends a diet that:

[22] Nelson, M. (1997). *Strong Women Live Longer.* NY: Ballentine Books.
[23] Hays, K. F. (2002). *Move Your Body Tone Your Mind.* Oakland, CA: New Harbinger.
[24] *Exercise: A Guide from the National Institute on Aging.* (Access it at www.nia.nih.gov/exercisebook)

- Incorporates a wide variety of foods daily;
- Is low in processed foods, saturated fat, cholesterol, sugar, and salt;
- Is rich in pasta, bread, fiber, vegetables, and fruits; and
- Contains no more than 30% of calories from fat in each day's intake.

The Department of Agriculture diet features a minimum of protein foods and dairy products. It provides the energy needed for active living and the reduction of stress. Breakfast "like a king," lunch "like a prince," and dinner "like a pauper," is an older but apt recommendation. These set the parameters for the recommended intake of the body's scheduled supply of nutrients. Eating a protein food for breakfast raises the blood sugar level, provides energy, and a sense of vitality. A balance is also necessary among proteins, fats, carbohydrates, vitamins, minerals, and water.

Unfortunately, many of us overload on fat, sugar, salt, caffeine, and alcohol. By doing so, we increase our risk for physical illness, stress, and mood changes. Instead, we need to consume nutritious food, which has sufficient fiber, water, and complex carbohydrates (fruit, grains, vegetables). According to the Center for Science in the Public Interest, the American high-caloric, high-fat, high sodium diet leads to health problems and obesity. Research indicates that poor diet and lack of exercise contribute to as many preventable deaths each year as smoking. Here are some suggestions for creating a more healthful diet:

- <u>Eat breakfast</u> – Sufficient protein, fiber, fats, carbohydrates, and sugars in the morning will power up energy level and alertness and will provide a jump on needed daily fiber. A breakfast that includes milk or yogurt, whole grains, and fruits improves alertness, strength, and endurance and reduces impulsive snacking of high fat and refined carbohydrate foods.

- <u>Eat healthy snacks</u> – Choosing to substitute some snacking for regular meals may offer nutrients to the body at a more appropriate rate. If snacks contain whole grains, fruits, nuts, and vegetables, they may also help to lower cholesterol.

- <u>Consider vegetarian meals</u> – Plant-based diets are generally low in calories and saturated fat and may fight chronic illness.

- <u>Drink six to eight glasses of water a day</u> – Water is essential for bodily functioning and prevents cramping during exercise.

- <u>Make eating a pleasure</u> – The social and aesthetic context of eating makes food intake relaxing and confers general health benefits. Eat slowly to experience satisfaction without overeating.

MAINTAIN A HEALTHY WEIGHT

Since eating is so much a part of family ritual, food can become entangled in blocking feelings and distorting experience. Eating "addiction" (a habituation) includes compulsive dieting, binge eating, bulimia, and anorexia nervosa.

Stanley J.Gross, Ed. D.

Being overweight, in and of itself is *not* an eating addiction. At this writing, 65 per cent of adult Americans are overweight and 31 percent are obese[25]. Overweight can be a precursor to obesity. Those who are obese (30 per cent or more above their ideal body weight) risk serious health complications. Recent estimates show the numbers of obese Americans increased from 12 per cent in 1991 to 18 percent of the population in 1998. An obese person is at a higher risk for heart disease, high blood pressure, stroke, diabetes, kidney and breathing problems, some cancers, and depression. It has been estimated that 300,000 Americans die each year because of the complications related to obesity.

The loss of 5 to 10 pounds by an obese person may be enough to improve blood pressure and diabetes conditions. Estimates[26] are that 30 minutes of moderate intensity exercise daily can improve health-related outcomes, but it takes at least 60 minutes of daily exercise at the same level to impact weight loss and prevent weight gain. Lowering health risks and improving fitness can foster appropriate, specific, and measurable goals for weight loss. The problem is that many people set a goal for achieving beauty as defined by cosmetic models or movie stars. The impossibility and generality of this goal doom the effort to failure. Because it is generated out of a negative view of oneself (for example, "I am not beautiful"), it elicits actions that are never enough because we are not "enough." Identifying specific health risks or fitness

---

[25] Foster, G.D. & Nonas, C.A. (2004). *Managing obesity: A Clinical Guide*. Chicago: American Dietetic Association.
[26] Jakicic, J.M. (2003). The Role of Exercise in the Management of Body Weight, *On the Cutting Edge, 24* (6) 30-32.

objectives makes success more likely. The plan might include these strategies:

- Have a reasonable weight loss goal (10%);
- Eat only when hungry, not when emotions call for comfort food;
- Eat meals at a regularly scheduled time;
- Reduce the amount of food eaten at each meal;
- Avoid snacks between meals or substitute healthy choices for current snacks;
- Maintain a diet emphasizing whole grain products, fruits, vegetables, low fat dairy food and meat over high fat meat, and processed foods;
- Exercise regularly (at least 3 times a week);
- Increase ordinary physical activity (park at a distance from destination and take the stairs);
- Get sufficient sleep; and
- Attend support groups or find a partner for self-care activities.

Developing a specific plan and keeping a food and exercise diary helps to spot needed changes. Many people report feeling better about their bodies' appearance with as little as a five percent weight loss. Laurel Mellin's, *The Diet-Free Solution*[27] and Walter C. Willett's *Eat, Drink and Be Healthy*[28] are helpful resources.

Consider a weight loss plan only when we are prepared to make a commitment to maintain it. Without

[27] Mellin, *Op. cit. (1998)*
[28] Willett, Walter C. (2001). *Eat, Drink, and Be Healthy: The Harvard Medical School Guide to Healthy Eating.* NY: Simon & Schuster.

commitment, there is a great likelihood of regaining the lost weight in a short time.

RELAXATION

Most of us need help to slow the quickened pace of our lives, having lost or never having had the gentle art of calming and centering. If we have the ability to elicit a "relaxation response," we become less reactive to stressful events. Some techniques were described previously in the self-soothing option. They include: "belly breathing;" shifting attention from the future or the past to the present; focusing on "being" rather than "doing;" and concentrating on internal rather than external matters. Since the mechanisms that affect stress are not directly accessible to the conscious mind, we focus on a centering technique that indirectly takes us to a calmer state. Centering includes self-soothing. It involves deliberately shifting our focus of attention so that we alter our awareness of our experience in the moment.

The following centering exercise features a meditation technique. Meditation is designed to encourage us to stop thinking (imagine that the brain stops working). Relaxation is achieved as part of the focus of attention on NOTHING. Follow these suggestions in order. (NOTE: Read the following instructions into a tape recorder to play them back to guide the meditation.)

1. Take time out. Arousal is a sign that you are not relaxed. Stop whatever you are doing or thinking. Centering is about nothing – no thinking, no working, and no planning.
2. Find a quiet place where you are not likely to be interrupted by people, noise, or smells.

3. <u>Get into a position</u> where discomfort will not interrupt your concentration.
4. <u>Choose a mental image</u> (a word, number, phrase, or visual picture) or your own breathing on which to focus;
5. <u>Close your eyes</u> when ready;
6. <u>Take slow and natural breaths</u>, focusing on an image;
7. <u>Acknowledge distracting thoughts</u> (which are normal) and go back to the focus; and
8. <u>Work up to following this procedure</u> 10 to 20 minutes, once or twice a day.

"Put It on the Shelf" Visualization

This visualization targets those times when a thought seems to "take over," and you have difficulty letting it go. It takes the centering technique described above one step further. Centering distracts your attention and brings it to an internal focus. Begin by following the first seven instructions in the above relaxation procedure. Continue here with suggestion number 9.

9. <u>Visualize</u> the persistent thought as a small object.
10. <u>Place</u> the object in a box.
11. <u>Imagine</u> a closet.
12. <u>Open</u> the closet door.
13. <u>Notice</u> the closet has a high shelf.
14. <u>Place</u> the object on the shelf.
15. <u>Tell</u> yourself that you do not need the thought now, but when you do it will always be available in the box on this shelf.
16. <u>Observe</u> that the box remains on the shelf.
17. <u>Close</u> the door.
18. <u>Return</u> to noticing your breathing – in and out.

19. <u>Open</u> your eyes when ready and acknowledge your surroundings.

Write about Concerns

If we enjoy writing, then taking up writing about life concerns will calm our bodies by reducing blood pressure and heart rate. Because of its empowering ability, writing can reduce anxiety and depression. Though it may not completely rid us of intrusive thoughts, self-expression reduces their negative impact. However, it is less likely that writing will help people who detest doing it.

Try this exercise. For four days, write about your deepest thoughts and feelings for 20 minutes. Just let it flow. Don't worry about grammar or spelling. Evaluate it after the four days to see if it helps you.

MAINTAIN HEALTHY SLEEP

Sleep is essential for positive physical and emotional health. Sufficient sleep (for most people seven to eight hours) meets our body's needs for rest and repair. Sleep rejuvenates by increasing alertness, receptivity, and concentration. Sleeping difficulties include problems of falling asleep, of waking repeatedly, and of failing to go back to sleep. These problems may result from stress, substance abuse, depression, illness, or genetic predisposition. Environmental irritants, such as noise, odors, and light, may also be factors in sleep problems. Personal habits, such as smoking, eating too close to bedtime, caffeine, worry, and lack of exercise, may be involved. If your sleep is often disturbed, consult your physician as it may have a physical basis.

Insufficient sleep poses an increased risk of irritability, excessive tiredness, substance abuse, heart trouble, digestive disease, and accidents. Reliance on sleeping pills can make sleep problems worse because of their decreasing effect with use. Attending to factors contributing to sleep problems includes:

- Avoiding alcohol, water, and cigarettes near bedtime;
- Eliminating caffeinated beverages within four hours of bedtime;
- Doing some exercise during the day but avoiding it within three hours of bedtime;
- Keeping your bedroom dark, cool, quiet, and free of cooking odors;
- Developing regular bedtime habits (for example, a regular bed time, using bed for sleep and sex only), and relaxing rituals;
- Seeing a physician if sleep problems persist.

MAINTAIN SEXUAL HEALTH

Sexuality is a source of excitement *and* pain, fulfillment *and* frustration. Sexual adjustment requires a knowledge base. Many people think they know more about sex than they do. As a result, misunderstanding and confusion are rife. The separation of sexuality from emotional intimacy is widespread, creating an industry around sexual exploitation, confusion about sexuality and relationships, and difficulties for many people about achieving coherent sexual and emotional intimacy. Secretiveness and shame often make communication about sexuality both awkward and distorted, retarding the flow of accurate information, and promoting myth and misinformation. Practicing safe sex, getting valid information, and participating in open discussion about sexuality promote sexual health.

Sudden increases or decreases of sexual interest or activity, promiscuity, and sexual dysfunction may be symptoms of stress or depression. In many ways, the lack of positive sexual health affects others as well as us. The threat of sexually transmitted disease is so great that there is personal danger in practicing unsafe sex. The sexual abuse of children and adult women is in epidemic numbers. This latter phenomenon is a distorted expression of power and dominance needs gone awry, leaving untold human suffering and maladjustment in its wake. Same-sex sexual identity can be confusing for teenagers, given the prejudice against those who follow a gay or lesbian lifestyle. Peer pressure, social attitudes, family rules, and cultural myths influence sexual expression.

MAINTAIN SPIRITUAL HEALTH

Spirituality connects our inner selves with something larger. For many people this means a formal association with a recognized religious institution. For others the practice may include Sunday morning TV ministries, religious self-help books, or New Age mysticism, such as feng-shui, crystal gazing, or angelolatry. Still others follow more individual or divergent paths involving such practices as meditation, spirituality-centered activism, and participation in spirituality-oriented communities. Whatever the practice, a common thread is the reaching out for meaning beyond our ordinary satisfaction-centered activities. When an ongoing spiritual connection is made, the sense of belonging is supportive and empowering. New ways of thinking and acting may be promulgated and absorbed, which enhance life experience.

The point was, where was all this anger coming from? Why was he being caught off guard, time and time again, by surges of rage that almost overwhelmed his will?

He took a cold shower. Then for two hours he lay in his darkened bedroom, with both air conditioner and ceiling fan working flat out to battle the heat and humidity. Controlling his breathing helped, and he also used visualization techniques to relax. He imagined the anger as a physical object, a soft, dark throbbing lump, and mentally drew a red triangle around it. Then he slowly made the triangle smaller, until the lump disappeared. It worked. His heart rate returned to normal.

– Salman Rushdie, "Summer of Solanka," *The New Yorker.* June 16, 2001. p.71.

We begin life with the world presenting itself to us as it is. Someone – our parents, teachers, analysts – hypnotize us to "see" the world and construe it in the "right" way. These others label the world, attach names and give voices to the beings and events in it, so that thereafter, we cannot read the world in any other language or hear it saying other things to us.

The task is to break the hypnotic spell, so that we become undeaf, unblind and multilingual, thereby letting the world speak to us in new voices and write all its possible meanings in the book of our existence.

Be careful in your choice of hypnotists. – Sidney Jourard

PART IV

I couldn't help myself.

SLOW IMPULSIVE RESPONDING

A different way of thinking is required to slow impulsive responses. As a result, some of the following material may be confusing. On Levels ❷ and ❸, we focused on "doing," that is, on specific self-caring actions. Level ❹ begins the shift to "being" where there is less emphasis on action and more emphasis on self-awareness. Some of us who are still struggling with addiction or self-care issues will have a harder time here. We may still be trying to control our inner experience with external substances or rituals. We may not know how to depend on our own resources for self-control. These are the goals of containment and initiating self-caring activities. To enhance our benefits from this program, a return to Level ❷ or ❸ is necessary, as Level ❹ requires being able to tolerate confusion and discomfort.

LEVEL ❹ directs us to awaken to our impulsive reactions. Here we can gain the tools and skills to slow our over reactions and address our negative beliefs. Reducing impulsivity will improve our choices about how to act in less self-defeating or self-destructive

123

ways. This permits us to value ourselves further with effective and self-caring actions. LEVEL ❹ choices raise our global self-esteem by increasing our inner control over our lives.

EVIDENCE OF PROGRESS

The pace of progress will be quicker than previous levels as long as we are not expecting magic. Again, diligence pays off with the following increases in skill:

- <u>Greater emotional distance from stressful circumstances</u> – By saying,"Hmm…I wonder what this is about," our impulsive, personalizing reactions occur less often. Instead, we delay our response, slowing down to choose to be more self-caring and effective.
- <u>Clarity about feelings</u> – Becoming more sensitive to where feelings occur in our body helps to identify and make clear their meaning.
- <u>Tolerate confusion</u> – Increased comfort to consider several choices at the same time.
- <u>Increased self-caring action</u> – We become more accepting of our imperfections and less tolerant of abuse from others as we take better care of ourselves.
- <u>Decreased aggression or submission</u> – We become more assertive and able to confront differences with others.
- <u>Reduced self-absorption</u> – We worry less about what others think of us as we become more aware of others as separate human beings with their own needs.

Chapter 11

PERSONALIZING AND THE LOSS OF CHOICE

Panic seized me. I longed to rip up my schedule and fill out a new one entirely in keeping with her wishes. If I didn't please this woman, she would withdraw her affection and support. On the other hand, if I didn't please myself, I might end up like my mother, sacrificed to others' whims for so long that I'd no longer know what I wanted.
– Lisa Alther, Kin-Flicks

It can happen in an instant. The transition from conversation to argument, from inaction to action, or from flexible to frozen occurs so quickly and the reaction is so intense that we can lose sight of what actually happened. Some triggering circumstance has caused us a great deal of discomfort. We "take offense." We believe the circumstance compromises us. It is a slur on our integrity. It threatens us. We *personalize* the situation.

The Immediate Effect of Threat

The immediate result of personalizing is discomfort from physical, cognitive, and emotional arousal. Physically, our heart rate, blood pressure, perspiration, and physical activity increase; our breath is faster and flatter; and our muscle tension heightens. Mentally, our attention is intently focused on the immediate crisis, while our thinking becomes disorganized. Emotionally, we may respond with a flood of feelings or shut down and feel nothing.

Emotional distancing and impulsive actions follow quickly. We become defensive. We put up an emotional "wall" between others and ourselves. We act impulsively, forgetting that action under pressure usually leads to self-defeating or self-destructive consequences. Threats originating in conversation, for example, can be quickly transformed into arguments, then mutual raging, icy silence, emotional abuse, or physical violence.

In the following vignette, Bette's triggering circumstance was not clear to her. Bette's habitual "racing her thoughts" had a trance-like quality with self-defeating and self-destructive consequences.

> *Bette had the habit of "racing" her thoughts, speech, and actions. Sometimes she talked so fast; people could not keep up with her. She could not remember a time when she did not act this way. So, when people commented on her behavior, she dismissed them as not understanding what was normal for her. She was competent at her job, but co-workers considered her "quirky." Her husband and children sometimes found her conduct annoying, but they, too, dismissed it as "that's Mom." One day, she had been talking at a particularly fast pace at a meeting with her supervisor about a problem in her work. He could not understand what she was saying and asked her to slow down. She was surprised by*

his request but dutifully tried to slow down. In a moment, she found herself welling up with feeling. It was as if a dam had burst. She began crying uncontrollably. For the first time, she realized how hard she was working not to feel her feelings.

Though she was aware of her "racing" behavior, Bette was unaware of its basis. She was mindless about it until her supervisor asked her to slow down. She was, however, already on edge, having interpreted the meeting to mean she was doing something wrong. When he, then, asked her to slow down, she could no longer contain her fears. Avoiding her fears and the belief in her inadequacy resulted in two consequences important to understanding low self-esteem.

- People with low self-esteem do not have a conscious choice when they act in their self-defeating or self-destructive ways. I call this inability to choose the *coping impulse trance.* The trance suppresses choosing. It has us repeating dysfunctional behavior in response to particular stressful circumstances that act as triggering events. These circumstances prompt a sense of shame. The shame preempts effective or self-caring action.

- The trance effectively blocked or distorted fears during our growing years. We avoided the natural lessons usually learned in family and school about how to deal with stressful events. Thus, we failed to develop the life skills we would need to deal with stress. I describe these as *insufficient life skills.* When in trance we neither know to choose, how to choose, or what to choose. A sense of helplessness and hopelessness prompts us to reach out and ask, "What should I do?" But, in trance, we do not integrate any advice we might hear. In this way, we repeatedly confirm our helplessness and hopelessness. We maintain the ineffective behavior and continue to reinforce our low self-esteem.

WHAT IS A TRANCE?

We are "on automatic," in a state of altered attention, a waking sleep, when in trance. Trances can have several characteristics: a trance may appear as intense concentration, as when we are absorbed by an exciting mystery novel; it may appear as a "spacing out," as when we are bored, and our attention flies out the window; or, trances may include repetitive "mindless" acts, which we do not think about since we perform them daily – like walking, brushing teeth, eating, etc. In any case, self-awareness is blocked.

Cues from our inner and outer worlds induce trances as pat responses. We associate these cues with prior experience. Examples might include the urge to go shopping following disappointment; a parent's rage reaction to disobedience; as well as the more benign expectation that when the family eats dinner together, father will say "grace." Much of human behavior is mindless. We react to many of life's circumstances in an automatic way. We do not give much thought to the choices we are making. Mindlessness has the effect of distancing us from what is happening.

Trances are not necessarily bad for us. They can help us to cope with stress and to simplify our lives in many ways. While driving, for example, the highway trance reduces stress by lessening the boredom and fatigue involved in long-distance driving. While many trances are benign, a trance may close out crucial options for us. The highway trance, which causes inattention in traffic, may lead to an accident. Though trances are useful in stress reduction, they may also be self-defeating, if they block achieving our goals, or self-destructive, if we become hurt or abused in some way.

WHERE DOES THE TRANCE COME FROM?

We come into this world ripe with potential and surging with capacities for life. We are unlike other mammals in two important ways. Relative to our size, we have a large and complex brain. Relative to our normal lifespan, we are dependent on adult caretakers for a long time. Because of these factors, we have a heightened capacity for learning, reflective thought, and choice. This means we have fewer instinctive responses. Our capacities make us prime candidates to develop uniquely with a variety of skills to face life's challenges.

The good news: Children receive three essential requirements for growth from their culture, social institutions, and adult caretakers. Appropriate limits, stimulation, and unconditional positive regard give them the ability to self-regulate, self-realize, and to make effective relationships. Everyone has these capabilities!

The bad news: Children do not receive these essential requirements due to neglect or abuse attributable to culture, social institutions, and adult caretakers. Robert Firestone's *Compassionate Child Rearing* and Alice Miller's, *For Your Own Good* document the culturally institutionalized cruelty to children done in the name of parenting. These books help us comprehend the widespread abuse and neglect we see in our world. Research reported in the *Journal of Clinical Child Psychology* in 1995 [29] showed that traumatic events are more widespread for children than commonly thought. Reports of extremes of physical, sexual, and emotional abuse, as well as severe deprivation and neglect are said to total in the millions yearly. In addition, there are more common forms of emotional abuse (for example: raging, spurning, isolating, ignoring, and exploiting) and neglect (lack of supervision and failure to provide).

When the abuse or neglect are coupled, as they usually are, with the inability to give voice to fears, the situation is ripe for developing the trance. Children depend on their adult caretakers and require assurance that their caretakers not abandon them. Abandonment appears a likely possibility to them, especially if they are subject to abuse or neglect. Since this prospect is too scary to think about, the trance distances them from the terror. Their capabilities for choice and development are then bent to the service of pleasing the caretakers. In a child's logic, the pain of abuse and neglect are worth it since they believe it prevents them from being

[29] Becker, J.V., Alpert, J., BigFoot, D.S., Bonner, B.L., Geddie, L.F., Henggler, S.W., Kaufman, K.L., & Walker, C. E. (1995). Empirical Research on Child Abuse and Neglect Treatment Working Group: American Psychological Association. *Journal of Clinical Child Psychology, 24* (Supplement) pp. 23-46.

abandoned. It does not matter, in the development of the trance, that the belief may be mistaken.

THE COPING IMPULSE TRANCE

As children we felt fear in our helplessness to deal with the abuse and neglect. We learned to hide emotionally in order to protect ourselves. After a while, it all went "underground." Our fears became encapsulated by the trance to avoid the chaos, rejection, criticism, and hurt. The repetition of these experiences, no way to talk about them, and believing we were responsible, had us conclude we were unworthy. We followed this assessment by punishing ourselves with self-defeating and self-destructive action. Avoiding fears in childhood by the retreat into trance broke the tie between these actions and the feelings and beliefs sustaining them. Avoiding fears blocked our emotional development.

As adults, without any awareness that we are protecting ourselves, we respond with confusion to adult equivalents of childhood abuse and neglect – criticism, conflict, rejection, and chaos. Confusion then evokes the trance. The part that confusion plays is to re-enact a terror previously felt at a younger age when we did not have the skills and resources to deal with neglect or abuse. As adults, when we avoid fear, we maintain the trance.

The coping impulse trance ritualizes automatic responses. Children miss opportunities to develop naturally the life skills required for self-care, detachment, optional thinking, assertion, and empathy. Learning how to approach confusion safely is also neglected. The trance continues to influence the growing child despite the actual decline in reliance

Stanley J.Gross, Ed. D.

upon caretakers. As adults, it occurs when we personalize situations and events

Personalizing Elicits the Coping Impulse Trance

We drink, we drug, we binge, we smoke, we rage, and we experience low self-esteem. Low self-esteem occurs as a consequence of taking responsibility for the abuse and neglect imposed on us as children by our caretakers. We do not do this consciously. Instead, it lurks as a hidden assumption, a throwback to that time in childhood when we saw ourselves as the center of the universe, and we were responsible for everything. We took the blame in a Faustian bargain. If we believed what we thought our abusive or neglectful caretakers wanted us to believe, then they would not abandon us.

Taking responsibility for our own abuse produced mistaken negative core beliefs that we continue to hold about our lack of lovability, inadequacy, shamefulness, or being wrong. We hold these ideas close to our hearts and hope others will not discover our secret. We live our lives deceiving ourselves that we do not believe these ideas. At the same time, we fear they will become public. Impulsive action follows immediately upon hearing criticism, rejection, or that we have made a mistake; because we fear our secret belief is revealed. By not facing these fears, they stay with us, multiply, and rot the core of our emotional selves.

Though we are unaware of the fear of exposure, covering up the secret produces an instant change from calm to impulse. The transition from normality to

132

crisis is so quick and so intense that we lose sight of everything except our fear. We take our supervisor's feedback as negative criticism. If a friend says "no" to our request, we see that as rejection. We feel compromised if we fail at a task. Criticism, rejection, and failure are all intolerable. . We perceive negative events as slurs on our integrity. We feel threatened. These situations become personalized.

The experience of personalizing includes confusion and discomfort resulting from physical, cognitive, and emotional arousal. Evident symptoms include: increases in heart rate, blood pressure, activity, and perspiration; breath is faster and flatter; and muscle tension heightens. Attention focuses on the immediate and thinking becomes disorganized. Feelings overwhelm us or are not felt at all.

Our subsequent impulsive action usually has immediate and long-range, self-defeating or self-destructive outcomes. At the moment it is likely we will rage or be silent. In extreme cases, impulsive action may trigger physical violence. When in the coping impulse trance, we are not aware that we have any options, other than to do what we have always done in such situations. We are rarely able to talk about how we feel in the moment.

Ingredients of an Inner Process

Virginia Satir[30] discovered an internal process that helps us to understand the coping impulse trance. Her insights suggest the trance follows a particular path. With awareness of this path, we can slow the

[30] *Op. cit. The New People Making.*

trance, detrance, and give ourselves new choices. The following ingredients of a trance (depicted in Diagram # 5) occur in the order presented in the diagram:

- **Perceiving** – Of all that may be seen and heard, we select out some of it for our attention. Because we base the selection on unmet emotional needs, biased and distorted perceptions often block accurate reception of what has actually happened. A fear of rejection may set us up to focus on cues that indicate inattention, or we may read a critical intent in what a friend intends as a compliment. In this way, we either deny what may be true, seeing only what we want to see, or assume we have heard something that was not said.

- **Meaning** – After we perceive something we attach meaning to it based on our core beliefs. This is the "spin" we put on what we have perceived. If, for example, we have the expectation that we should be perfect, we will likely believe we are "bad" or "wrong" if we think we have made a mistake. We, then, may assume we are victims, since mistakes seem to seek us out.

- **Feeling about meaning** – Feelings are always about something. After we attach a meaning to an event, feelings follow. In the coping impulse trance, our feelings are vague and confusing, if we feel anything. We may experience frustration, tension, guilt, anxiety, shame or nothing at all.

- **Feelings about the feeling** – Rules influence the acceptability of our feelings. In our families, we learned rules about what is permissible to feel. We become defensive, because we have been taught that what we feel is not acceptable. When this occurs, we are likely to stifle our feelings.

*   **Coping style** – If feelings are not acceptable, we develop a negative attitude. This attitude governs the type of response we will make to the stressful event. The following represent four possible attitudes we may choose to cope with threats to our integrity.

    ☐ **Blaming** – With the stance of blaming others, we shift responsibility for threatening events away from us. Despite concern about others' opinion, avoiding responsibility has a higher priority. We hope to protect ourselves from expected accusations. We think a good offense is the best defense. Forms of blaming include: discounting, stonewalling, contempt, hostility, nagging, demanding, attacking, abusing, or criticizing.

    ☐ **Placating** – With the stance of taking responsibility for threatening events, we hope to keep the peace and avoid the expected anger of others. We are led to give our personal power away. We avoid confrontation, become anxious, appease others, allow abuse, discount our needs, place others before ourselves, accept blame that is not ours, and give in to unreasonable demands.

AN EXTERNAL (BECKONING) EVENT OCCURS
1. A demanding event occurs. We are confused & fearful.↓

Inner Process		
Coping Trance	**↓**	**Intuitive**
	Perception	
2. Distorted – focus denies or twists event.	*(Based on needs)* ↓	2. Accurate – focus on event as problem.
	Meaning	
3. Rigid and dualistic – "Spin" personalizes event.	*(Based on core beliefs)* ↓	3. Fitting – "Spin" is "bad things happen; learn something."
	Feeling about meaning	
4. Overwhelmed or frozen – tense, frustrated, shamed.	*(Based on access to feelings)* ↓	4. Perceptive – feel mad, glad, sad, or scared.
	Feeling about feeling	
5. Negative – Not OK to feel this way.	*(Based on family rules)* ↓	5. Positive – It is OK to feel.
	Coping style	
6. Defensive – blame or placate, deny, be irrelevant	*(Based on attitudes)* ↓	6. Open – assert self, receptive, thoughtful, creative.
	Rule about commenting	
7. Negative – Can't talk about event.	*(Based on family rules)* ↓	7. Positive – right to talk about this.

EXTERNAL REACTIONS TO EVENT

Coping impulse	Choice
8. I act impulsively. My actions are self-defeating.	8. I am self-aware - I trust myself. I ask for what I want..

Diagram # 5 – Ingredients of an Inner Process [31]

[31] Derived from the work of Virginia Satir (Satir, et al., 1991)

☐ **Intellectualizing** – The intellectualizing stance diffuses responsibility for threatening events. We are led to act "super-rationally." Thus, we gain distance from our uncomfortable feelings. We focus on the rational; we try to sound "intelligent;" we lecture; and we behave "appropriately."

☐ **Irrelevance** – The stance of shifting attention to the illogical creates confusion about who is responsible for what. We act oddly and gain distance from our uncomfortable feelings. We are led to act like clowns and become the center of attention. We distract others by interrupting, act erratically, behave inappropriately, do several things at once, or shift from one topic to another.

Rule about commenting – Rules learned in our families control the suitability of talking to the offending person in the stressful situation. The rule can block sharing entirely or until after arousal passes.

The following is an example of a coping impulse trance:

> *A mathematics professor in his fifties, who likes to think of himself as dynamic and rakish but who is, at the moment, "between lovers," stands on the subway platform eyeing an undergraduate. He sees that his gaze is making her uncomfortable. He feels a twinge of shame over this intrusion but not enough to stop. He files his behavior under "manly aggression" and keeps staring. Then, a searing thought enters and exits his mind so*

fast that later he won't remember having had it. The idea seems almost to have been waiting there like a hot coal, and, after stumbling upon it and getting singed, he flees in panic. Feeling inexplicably crestfallen, he looks away from the young woman, buries his head in his paper, and seeks out a separate car when the train comes in. For the rest of the morning he feels listless and down. He doesn't want people near him and growls if they press. He works methodically, waiting for the unnamable discomfort to pass. The idea that scorched him was an image of himself, all too believable, as a hungry, unhappy loner, a man who had wasted his youth and was incapable of lasting attachments, staring forlornly at a woman who could not possibly be interested in him.[32]

Using Satir's outline, the professor sexualizes the "encounter." A moment after perceiving the young woman's discomfort, his core belief that he is a despicable loner comes to dominate his thinking. His fear of intimacy is not acceptable. His attitude is to blame himself, a placating response. It is, of course, not acceptable to him to talk to anyone about the incident, which is why at fifty he continues to behave like a teenager. This incident also illustrates how self-defeating action results from the trance.

[32] Robert Karen, "Shame." *The Atlantic Monthly*, February 1992, p. 40.

Chapter 12

SELF-REGULATION SKILLS

Cheryl, a 29-year-old woman, grew up in an alcoholic family. Self-esteem was one of her several problems. She began our second session saying, "Well, I did it." Upon my asking what she did, she told me about ending the relationship with her married lover. It turned out that her shame about the relationship (which she had not referred to in our first session) led her to see it as self-abusing. Perhaps, it was our discussion during the first session about saying "no" to her emotionally abusive mother that motivated her. Whatever it was, ending the relationship represented her first step in establishing herself as a separate person. Her progress during the next few months was more complicated, but saying "no" to him and "yes" to herself was a crucial beginning.

Cheryl's self-abusive relationship connects low self-esteem to the absence of a clear sense of boundaries. People with low self-esteem often have other insufficient self-regulatory skills associated with low self-esteem. They tend to:

- See danger rather than opportunity when facing new or problem situations;

- Lack awareness of options other than those they routinely choose;
- Think about these events in "all or none" categories;
- Find their feelings frighten them rather than aid in their problem solving;
- Have difficulty with assertion instead are submissive or aggressive;
- Expect to see negative outcomes for their efforts.

People with low self-esteem, as previously discussed in Chapters 1, 2 and 11, have fended off a mix of neglect, indifference, and abuse in their childhood. As a result, they did not learn essential self-regulatory skills when it was appropriate to do so. In their adult years, new or problem incidents foster reenactments of childhood abuse or neglect. Their responses reflect extremes in thinking, feeling, and action (for example, they are overwhelmed by their feelings or feel nothing). Since these responses did not fit their current circumstances, the outcome becomes self-defeating or self-destructive. Their self-esteem plummets. Their dysfunctional actions represent *insufficiencies of self-regulatory skill.*

SELF-REGULATION SKILL DOMAINS

The level of our self-esteem is indicated by six categories of self-regulation skill (See Diagram # 6). The following skill domains are described later in this chapter:

- Action – The degree to which we have command over our own behavior.

- Feelings – Our involuntary internal reactions to our experience.
- Thinking – How we derive meaning from our experience.
- Boundaries – Our emotional separations from others.
- Control – Our experience of power in relationships.
- Receptivity – The extent to which we are open to others and new experience.

LEVELS OF SELF-REGULATION SKILLS

In this formulation, each domain has five levels of development. The <u>first</u> level of each domain represents an absence of ability or *skill insufficiency*. These are the minimal coping skills we had when we were young children. We resort to these skills when we are stressed. As adults this level represents the ways we abuse ourselves. Higher levels show increased ability or *skill sufficiency*. At the <u>second</u> level we are aware of the skill insufficiency but are not ready to do anything about it. This is when we ask others, "What should I do?" The <u>third</u> level begins the life style self-care changes that jump-start increases in self-esteem. At the <u>fourth</u> level we are concerned with slowing our reactivity to events and to others. The <u>fifth</u> level is when we untie our reactions from the abuse and neglect of childhood. This high degree of self-regulatory skill permits us to define life events for ourselves rather than allowing others to do them for us. In this way, we learn to rely on our own personal resources to determine our destiny. As we increase our level of skill sufficiency, we become more proficient in dealing with life's dilemmas.

Low Self-Esteem   **Positive Self-Esteem**

SKILL INSUFFI-CIENCY	EXPRESSED IN EXTREMES	SKILL DOMAINS	SKILL SUFFICIENCY	INTEGRATED IN DAILY BEHAVIOR
Impulsive Responses	Over/under reacts; angry or withholding.	ACTION	Considered Responses	Slowed reaction; choice & action are positive & fitting.
Emotional Uncertainty	Overwhelming, or frozen feelings.	FEELING	Emotional Clarity	Names & values feelings and messages.
Dualistic Thinking	Confusion not OK; thinking right/wrong.	THINKING	Optional Thinking	Confusion OK, sees multiple & relative options.
Enmeshed	Fused or aloof; allows abuse, poor self-care.	BOUNDARIES	Detached	Keeps limits, allow differences; self-caring; takes help.
Control-oriented	Dominates, manipulates, or submissive.	CONTROL	Assertive	Has right to meet needs; acts directly, & speaks honestly.
Closed	Blocks or skews feedback worries, pretends.	RECEPTIVITY	Open	Gets accurate feedback; responsive.

Diagram # 6 – Self-Regulatory Skill Domains

142

It is important to evaluate one's level of skill sufficiency accurately. Awareness of our skill level helps us to initiate the most appropriate action to raise it. Hoping we will be seen or see ourselves as more advanced than we are blocks this. Such self-appraisals are exercises in self-deception. The distortion is usually self-limiting as it is difficult for many of us to understand fully a skill more than one level above our own actual skill level.

SKILL DOMAIN: ACTION

Action Involves The Degree of Command We Have Over Our Behavior.

Impulsive reactions typify low self-esteem. These automatic responses generally are self-defeating or self-destructive. When asked, people report they could neither control these responses nor explain what "made" them act as they did. This "mindless" response contrasts with *spontaneity*, which bases action on self-knowledge, awareness of circumstances, and choice. The more actions are self-generating, the more they meet our needs and are appropriate to the circumstances of our lives. Each of five levels listed below indicate a stepwise increase in action skill sufficiency.

LEVEL ❶	I am often impulsive.
LEVEL ❷	I don't know why I do the things I do.
LEVEL ❸	I don't have to act on my urges.
LEVEL ❹	I slow myself down to examine my options.
LEVEL ❺	I act respectfully and effectively.

SKILL DOMAIN: FEELINGS

Feelings Are Involuntary Internal Sensations.

Feelings are our bodies' responses to internal and external events. They serve as our early warning system. They contain information derived from our perceptions of life situations. The greater the variety of feelings we sense, the more variable are the messages we hear, the options we perceive, and the actions we can take. Thus, feelings are the basis of choice about what actions we take. With low self-esteem, we have difficulty regulating our emotions. Our feelings are either overwhelming or unavailable. *Emotional flooding* describes heightened feeling arousal.

We experience feelings in our bodies keenly, as immediate, compelling, and confusing. Symptoms of physical arousal (faster heart beat, sweating, etc.) and cognitive arousal (narrowed attention and disorganized thinking) intensify the effect of being threatened. Experiencing feelings may be delayed, blocked, or frozen.

With positive self-esteem, we appreciate our feelings. This means we are aware of and can name our feelings, differentiate them in our bodies, and understand what they are about. All of this information helps us to know ourselves and choose our actions. Each of five levels listed below indicate a stepwise increase in emotional skill sufficiency.

LEVEL ❶	I don't get emotional.
LEVEL ❷	I mostly don't know what I feel.
LEVEL ❸	I am coming to know what I feel.
LEVEL ❹	I feel my feelings in my body.
LEVEL ❺	I rely on my feelings to know what to do.

SKILL DOMAIN: THINKING

Thinking is how we derive meanings from our experience.

In low self-esteem thinking is *dualistic.* This primitive form of thought couches issues as either one meaning or its extreme opposite. Either/or thinking protects us from confusion by limiting our alternatives. By allowing extremes only, <u>dualistic</u> thinking recasts ambiguity and uncertainty into simple terms. As self-esteem increases, we become comfortable with more varied meanings. First, we consider options to either/or meanings. By thinking in <u>multiples,</u> we consider alternate meanings but not in any order of desirability. Then, when thinking <u>relatively,</u> we consider alternate meanings according to our principles, values, or goals. Flexibility permits more accuracy in meaning and greater effectiveness in choices. Finally, thinking <u>dialectically</u> permits reframing to consider the unusual. In dialectical thinking, our thought is holistic, and we are comfortable with paradox. Each of five levels listed below indicate a stepwise increase in thinking skill sufficiency.

LEVEL ❶	I am disturbed by disagreement.
LEVEL ❷	I see things as either right or wrong.
LEVEL ❸	I avoid extreme opinions.
LEVEL ❹	I think about a variety of opinions.
LEVEL ❺	I consider options according to my goals

SKILL DOMAIN: BOUNDARIES

Boundaries Create a Needed Emotional Separation of One Person From Another.

Boundaries, the recognition of the difference between "I" and "you," provide the basis for the willingness and ability to say "no," when appropriate. After all, our unique needs may be quite different from those with whom we are close. So, we require the ability to say "no" when we perceive something is not in our best interest. With low self-esteem, we are enmeshed or keep others at arm's length. Having few limits, the distinction blurs between "us" and "them." This, in turn, permits, on one hand, ignoring limits, tolerating abuse, poor self-care, or, on the other, isolation. Without boundaries we feel unsafe, thus we may alternate between losing ourselves in relationships or becoming isolated. Positive self-esteem includes the ability to detach emotionally. This includes the ability to say "no," reach out for help to others when needed, accept differences with others, and tolerate our own imperfections. We are able to trust that we will be "OK" in intimate relationships. Each of five levels listed below indicate a stepwise increase in boundary skill sufficiency.

LEVEL ❶	I say "yes" even if I don't mean it.
LEVEL ❷	I dislike saying "no" and hearing it from others.
LEVEL ❸	I say "no" to others when I need to.
LEVEL ❹	I say "yes" when it is the right thing to do.
LEVEL ❺	I trust some people to know the "real" me.

SKILL DOMAIN: CONTROL

Control Describes the Experience of Power in Relationships.

With low self-esteem, our history of helplessness with powerful people sets us up to believe we either control others or they control us. This belief assumes that power is outside of us and we must grab it or else we will lose. A rigid focus or distractibility characterizes our perception of events. We may think that *dominating* others proves we are not powerless. We desire to win, to have mastery, to be "in charge" in order to feel safe. *Submissive* behavior seeks to manipulate those whom we believe control us. We believe we cannot survive on our own. Fearing blame, we give our power away, placate, or become reactive and passive. Our needs go "underground." We may become "martyrs" or passive-aggressive. Positive self-esteem involves *assertion*. We believe we have a right to act in our own interest. Assertion involves self-control rather than the control of others. We are able to ask for what we want, make "I" statements, and negotiate differences with others. Each of five levels listed below indicate a stepwise increase in control skill sufficiency.

LEVEL ❶	I have to be in charge of things.
LEVEL ❷	I know I can't really control people.
LEVEL ❸	I curb trying to control others.
LEVEL ❹	I face differences with others.
LEVEL ❺	I balance what I want with what others want.

Stanley J.Gross, Ed. D.

SKILL   RECEPTIVITY

Receptivity Reflects Our Openness to Information.

The more receptive we are, the more information we have to make life decisions. The clearer and more inclusive our awareness, the better we are able to attend to our own needs and the needs of others. In low self-esteem, we are self-absorbed or worried. We alternate between everything being about us to worrying about negative possibilities. In positive self-esteem, we are attuned to our needs and the surrounding circumstances. We are aware of the contribution we make to events. We can listen to others speak of their needs without their requiring our action. We are sensitive our own body's cues and receptive to social cues from others. We act in our own interest by being self-caring yet can experience empathy. Each of five levels listed below indicate a stepwise increase in receptive skill sufficiency.

LEVEL ❶	I take care of number one.
LEVEL ❷	I disregard anything but my own needs.
LEVEL ❸	I listen to what others say about themselves.
LEVEL ❹	I consider what others need from me.
LEVEL ❺	I meet people halfway.

Chapter 13

UNLOCKING THE SECRET

The very common human act of mindless reactions to events in our lives, usually only has the effect of distancing ourselves from our experience. In fact, if we had to be mindful about everything we did, our lives could become, in John Dewey's words, "A booming, buzzing confusion." There are automatic reactions, however, which distort our experience and lead to much distress. Since we are mindless about it, its existence within us becomes an unintentional secret.

We are mindless when we personalize the stressful events occurring in our lives. We make stressful events about "us" rather than view them, as *just happening to happen* or reflecting the needs of others. We do this to protect a secret we believe is dangerously close to becoming known, even though we do not know we are doing this. We react quickly to suppress the secret, but it is always there, ready to surface. This secret is one we share with a host of others who have low self-esteem, but we also do not know that.

THE SHARED SECRET

Once upon a time, when they were quite small, some children were abused or neglected. They may have been physically beaten, yelled at, sexually fondled, overindulged, rejected, or ignored. Their

149

caretakers were likely so self-absorbed they may not have intended to abuse or neglect them. Nor did they realize the impact of their actions on the growing child. Nonetheless, the callousness, malevolence, cruelty, or insensitivity of their actions had an unintended and negative impact. With their emotional needs unmet and being unable to talk to anyone about what was going on, the children were confused and frightened. Since it happened repeatedly, they assumed, as children do, that the abuse or neglect was their fault. It was their punishment for doing something wrong. In thrall to this belief, they began to treat themselves as they had been treated and buried the secret of their wrongdoing deep into memory. Now, when events threaten to reveal their secret blame, they block the fear and confusion by victimizing themselves. They repeatedly and impulsively overreact, usually with self-abusing results.

THE ORIGINS OF LOW SELF-ESTEEM

When children do not receive what they need for emotional growth from their families, the result is low global self-esteem. The required conditions include: (1) clear yet flexible limits, (2) sufficient but not excessive stimulation, and (3) unconditional positive regard. When families do not provide these conditions, it results from sometimes unintentional neglect or abuse. We read in research reports[33] and

---

[33] Becker, J.V., *et al.*, *Op. cit.*

in our newspapers about extremes of physical, sexual, and emotional abuse of children, as well as severe deprivation and neglect totaling in the millions yearly. Also, "milder" forms of emotional abuse and neglect abound. Examples include: not being seen as having needs different from one's parents, being repeatedly criticized, lack of affection, no supervision, and being overindulged.

When early abuse and neglect link with limited opportunity for children to voice their fear about what they do not understand, the fear moves underground. Not being able to talk, children have nothing but their own limited information and their imagination to rely upon in grasping the meaning of events. Children also consider themselves the center of the universe. Unfortunately, this carries with it the responsibility for everything that goes on in that universe. The suppression of fear, the limitation of options, and the sense of being responsible cause these children to blame themselves for being abused and neglected. This is the basic misinterpretation that is at the core of low self-esteem.

Children come to believe they are at fault for abuse and neglect perpetrated by

> A child's talent to endure stems from the absence of alternatives.
> – Maya Angelou

their adult caretakers. Since the abuse or neglect could not be discussed, they assume, as children will, the abuse or neglect is their fault. They are confused and frightened. They bury the secret of their supposed wrong doing deep into memory. Their self-blaming not only remains underground, it is expressed in self-punishment and forms the basis for continuing mistaken interpretations. Also, since subsequent negative events threaten to expose the secret of their wrongdoing, they react automatically to suppress it. It remains, however, ever ready to surface. Now, when events threaten to reveal their secret, they block the resulting fear and confusion by overreacting, despite self-abusing results. Repeating this scenario numerous times over the course of years creates the self-punishment and shame we know as low self-esteem.

Early in our childhood we appreciate the importance of our adult caretakers. Without clarification, their abuse and neglect carries with it the implication that we are unworthy and deserve to be abandoned. That prospect is too scary to think about. So we learned to hide emotionally in order to protect ourselves. Our capabilities for choice and development were bent to the service of pleasing our caretakers rather than growth and learning. So, we assume, incorrectly, if the caretaker is abusing or neglecting us, it must be because we are unworthy and deserve it. Therefore, agreeing with the caretaker's view of us is thought to please them, in our child's logic. At this time we think we are who our caretakers think we are. So, it is not a large step for us to believe we are worthless and deserve to be abandoned by our caretakers. Thus, we not only punish ourselves by taking blame for our own abuse and neglect, we steel ourselves for the coming abandonment and take on the belief we are worthless. This is the belief at the core of low self-esteem.

We bury the memory of our fault and our wrongdoing. It becomes our secret. If we acknowledge it, then we will re-expose ourselves to the terrors attached to the helplessness and abandonment lodged deep in our memory. The secret, then, prevents us from re-evaluating our assumptions. The self-blaming and belief in our worthlessness are maintained despite evidence to the contrary. "Don't confuse me with the facts, my mind is made up," is the watchword. Subsequently, we believe we are responsible for all our negative experiences, despite the reality that these are random or the responsibility of others. We judge ourselves harshly. We keep punishing ourselves because of these judgments. None of this comes into awareness, because we act impulsively to any event that might dislodge the secret from its protected place in our memory. These automatic reactions result in self-defeating or self-destructive consequences that punish us again and again. After a while, the threatening events became triggers for eliciting a sense of shame instead of the terror and the secret of our wrongdoing remains underground. The secret covers our impulsive reactions and avoids the sensed rejection, criticism, hurt, and fear of abandonment. An overview of the steps in the development of low self-esteem is detailed in Diagram # 7.

PROGRAMMING THE TRANCE

Repeatedly, we hear of people who seem to have it all. They have achieved fame, riches, and admiration. However, we discover some feel miserably about themselves and have abusive or erratic relationships. What is happening here?

Our behavior in different situations depends on the context. Unless we have achieved a good deal of self-awareness, current and past associates influence us. Peers and mentors are most important in work, school, and social situations. Childhood experience in our families shapes behavior in close and intimate relationships. In these more personal settings, we often talk, walk, eat, and think like our parents or their

Diagram # 7 – Low Self-Esteem Pyramid

mirror opposites. Nevertheless, similar or opposite, our parents influence us. We often do not realize how influential they have been until we see similarities in the way we deal with our own children. Recognizing their influence on opposite behavior is more difficult.

We carry our childhood family around with us in a "family culture." This culture includes our knowledge, expectations, and attitudes about the world and how to act within it. Family culture became a part of us in our childhood as the result of observing and interacting with our parents. What we learn in the early years, called our "programming," becomes the yardstick against which we measure subsequent experience. Susan's experience in her family created a number of expectations, which are central to her problem with John. John, for his part, has differing expectations associated with *his* family.

> *Susan is the mother of six-month-old twin girls. She and her husband, John, had been married for three years before her difficult pregnancy. They expected the girls to be a "handful," so they decided that Susan would stay home for the first year and John would be the only family wage earner. Susan does not mind having to manage on her own during the day but finds it exasperating that John goes to AA (Alcoholics Anonymous) meetings in the evening, just when there is lots to do at home. She would like him to stay with her in the evening and help with the girls. Her resentment over his lack of responsiveness to her pleas is beginning to express itself in an old problem for her – excessive credit card spending.*

> Susan was the fourth in a family of eight children. Her father was an abusive alcoholic. Her mother and the children lived in fear of his rages. Her mother was so busy with her father and her younger siblings that she left much of Susan's care to her older sisters. Susan resolved she would never be as passive or neglectful as her mother. Now, she gets angry and rages at her husband when he is not at home to help her. When that does not work to get what she wants, she gets even by going shopping, despite their large credit card debt. On the way home with her packages, she feels a sense of shame. She realizes her anger and shopping are similar to her father's rages and alcoholism. She interprets John going to AA when she needs him to help her as his not caring. This connects with her belief that she is not important to him just as she was unimportant to her parents.

Susan's expectations about gender roles are driven by her place as a middle child in a chaotic, alcoholic family. Needing so much, she takes on aspects of her parents' dysfunctional behavior. She is intolerant of differences, rages at her husband, and finds an addictive solution to her neediness. John's rigidity and insensitivity to her needs stirs her rage. Neither one has a positive model of a couple talking calmly about problems.

Using the computer as a metaphor helps to visualize the nature of programming. Programming is similar to the "default" mode in the software of a computer. The common definition of default refers to failure. In computer terminology, default refers to arranging things to operate repeatedly and automatically. Computer default might be thought of as "failing choice." The computer has software, which is programmed to respond automatically whenever a particular cue arises. For example, each time we open a document it appears with the same font and type size.

Our personal programming operates in a similar way. From observing and interacting with our parents, their family culture becomes part of us. A pundit once said, "Children have nothing to do other than study their parents." What we learn in these early years takes on an inflexible character about which we seem to have little choice. During childhood and young adulthood, we test and re-test our programmed learning, opting to replicate it or reject it. Few of us have the sophistication or self-awareness to do anything but the opposite of our parents or, more likely, adopt peer culture as the model for our behavior. Nonetheless our family culture serves as the framework for our lives.

We continue to look to others for behavior models until life events allow (or force) us to consider options. Impulsive reactions to stressful events and conflict with others can bring this to light, if we are alert to the possibility. Automatic reactions often occur when we are exposed to stress from criticism, rejection, "put downs," or failure. Some self-awareness is necessary to recognize these events and see the opportunity to try fresh approaches to life dilemmas. An impediment is that choice appears risky and confusing.

Returning to the computer metaphor, we can easily change the font or the size of the type by overriding the default mode or by creating a new default. Our personal programming, though it too operates automatically, does not change that easily. We can change it, but it requires repeated overriding. To do this, we work on becoming aware of our family culture each time it surfaces in our behavior. With awareness, we gain the chance to choose to do something more effective and more self-caring.

Three components of family culture help us to understand the source of the expectations, which govern our day-to-day actions:

- Roles, or the dimensions we play in our life with others;
- Family rules, which guide "appropriate" action; and
- Core beliefs, or the thoughts underlying our acts and feelings, which provide the standards against which we evaluate our experience and ourselves.

ROLES

When asked, "Who are you?" we respond, "Mother, man, actor, teacher, student." Or, if we are more forthright, we may say, "alcoholic, achiever, lone wolf, loser." None of these designations describe who we *are*. Rather, they identify what we *do*. The words used are roles, which are defined as positions in social relations to which expectations become attached. As such, roles affect how we act in many of the circumstances of our lives. Roles are the parts we play on our life stage. The scripts or expectations for these dimensions are often unwritten but widely known (for example, how to be a man or a woman).

We learn how to act according to these roles while growing up in our families and from our peers and mentors. Our social and functional roles define what is appropriate.

Social roles are expectations for behavior for a labeled *formal* position in society (for example, woman, brother, doctor, janitor).

Functional roles are expectations for behavior for a labeled *informal* position in social interaction (for example, hustler, hero, sad sack, nerd).

Expectations for these roles direct us by indicating what behavior is appropriate and what is not. Roles provide the unthinking and stereotyped ways we behave in many situations. Situations also influence how roles become interpreted. One way of becoming aware of role behavior is to note how our behavior changes as we move from one situation to another, such as when we leave our friends to meet our parents. We move from one role (friend) to another (child) as we change situations.

Acting in these roles may be at odds with our personal desires. Roles, thus, impose a degree of control over us. For example, we are rewarded in some settings for being in the "good student" role and in other settings for the "bad student" role. Much of this control goes on outside of our awareness. We may not be conscious that our immediate behavior is influenced by our roles.

In countless situations, we see people interpreting roles in rigid or mindless ways. For example, some women assume they *have* to be responsible for everything about their marital relationship. Some men assume they *have* to be the primary breadwinners. Given these expectations, with no awareness they are merely expectations, they become demands. Disregarding these demands is an option, but the parties pay a cost. Shame, guilt, or conflict may occur following the failure or inability to fulfill these demands. It takes some flexibility to see that there may be various ways to define role expectations in marital relationships.

Our lack of awareness of options affects much of our intimate behavior. This is the hold our family of origin has over us. Of course, the roles lose a lot of their power to control our behavior when we become aware of them. This is why becoming aware of the roles influencing our behavior and clarifying the alternatives unleashes a powerful force for change.

FAMILY RULES

Family rules give us explicit guidance about how to act in social situations. Rules are designed to maintain communication, prevent aggression, and achieve cooperation. Instances include when we say the words or imply "should, must, always, or never." Similarly, when we feel discomfort with something new or different, we are likely to have a family rule in the background. Examples are, "always be nice, don't cry, get even, be on time, never make mistakes, and respect your elders." Teenagers often adopt personal rules that conflict with family rules.

Whatever the content of the rules, all social groups reinforce their rules with a variety of rewards and punishments. In response to being hurt in a fall, for example, a parent may commend us for our "stiff upper lip" if we do not cry or shame us if we do. In some families, there are teaching stories told about people who positively or negatively exemplify the rules parents' value. Was there a Jamie who could do no wrong in your family? Or, was there a "black sheep" named Noah?

Many families keep secrets, maintain rituals, and observe taboos that implicitly teach basic rules. A child's observation of parental behavior is a powerful teacher. The parents' actions in response to stress, problem solving, relationships, addiction, etc. becomes what "should" be done, despite of what parents "say." This especially applies to important family issues, including the use of money; the handling of discipline; the expression of feelings, sexuality, and affection; the experience of spirituality; and the treatment of people who are different racially or culturally. Childhood experience with these issues is the basis for rules followed or rejected in later relationships.

CORE BELIEFS

Personalizing describes the way we impulsively turn negatively perceived events into the shame we know as low self-esteem. Events appear as solely "about us." For example, we hear feedback about our actions as criticism. We assume the person has said we are inadequate, rather than seeing the feedback as useful information. If we make a mistake, we assume we are stupid, rather than seeing the failure as an opportunity to learn something. These personalized meanings are based on our negative core beliefs.

By avoiding fear we keep our negative core beliefs underground and our secret about our responsibility safe from unraveling. The continuing diet of impulsive overreacting and self-punishment validate these core beliefs. This is a closed circle. Structured this way, our secret is the key pin in a cul-de-sac that keeps us trapped. Since our negative core beliefs are central to maintaining the structure, the secret is vulnerable to awareness and information. The problem is to gain awareness and information to challenge the secret.

Core beliefs are used to classify and understand life events. By so doing, core beliefs validate our actions and form the basis for self-evaluation. In our families we develop core beliefs as we attempt to meet our emotional needs. The more our needs are met in childhood, the more positive our core beliefs (for example, "I am enough"). Negative core beliefs arise out of our difficulty in so doing (for example, "I am unlovable").

Core beliefs have their origins in childhood when we believe we are the center of the universe. Our naive way of thinking makes us responsible for everything that happens around us. If the adults in our families were consistent, responsible, and loving, we could talk to them about the events in our lives. This would have supported our growing sense of self and lead us to develop positive core beliefs, optimistic attitudes, a willingness to try new things, and the ability to learn from our experience.

Some families, however, were chaotic, arbitrary, cold, abusive, negative, neglectful, or conflicted. There was no adult to encourage, challenge, and

> For years I assumed responsibility for all that happened in my life, even for events over which I had not the slightest control.
> – Paula Fox [34]

[34] Whose Little Girl Are You? *New Yorker*, July 2, 2001, p. 55.

limit or talk appropriately about what was happening. Children find such conditions overwhelming. Children are too frightened to talk about their fears. They cannot distinguish between the negative outcome of an event and their responsibility for it. We heard, for example, "You are a bad boy (or girl)." We thought, "I am bad." Since we place our survival ahead of our emotional needs, we avert fear of our parents' abandonment of us by the mistaken notion that our actions *had* to please them. We tried out various behaviors and noticed it pleased them when we thought we were "bad." The resulting negative core belief about our "badness" is based on this perceived necessity. Though it is the product of an immature logic and is mistaken, we continue into adulthood believing it to be true. Mistaken core beliefs are no different from any other belief. They influence what events mean, how we feel about them, and how we react. Thus, they determine what we find threatening and stimulate us to personalize certain events in our lives.

The Dialectic Process

Many years ago, I attended a workshop on a self-help method called "Re-evaluation Counseling." Early in the workshop we met in groups of six to participate in a ritual in which each of us, in turn, would look at our face in the mirror and boast about ourselves while the others surrounded us in a tight circle. As each person performed this act, not more that ten seconds would elapse before the boaster was crying. Though the stated purpose of the technique was to stimulate catharsis for inner pain, this circumstance tells us something more about how core beliefs can be managed positively.

We release energy to raise our self-esteem when we are open about our beliefs. The way it works is called *The Dialectic Process.* This natural process occurs when we make any all-inclusive statement such as, "I believe I am unlovable." Upon making the statement our attention turns automatically to what the statement does *not* include, for example, "Mother loved me." In this way, our negative statement about ourselves is no sooner said than we become aware of what is not included – its' positive opposite. Our positive statements similarly call out their negative opposites. Affirmation statements such as, "I am a lovable person" turn into "I am unlovable" and do not help us raise our self-esteem.

We *want* to erase our negative core beliefs. Unfortunately, the harder we work at it, the more tenaciously these beliefs cling to us. They represent what we mistakenly thought we had to believe in order to please our caretakers or what we believed we needed to think in order to survive in the abusive/ neglectful environment of our family of origin. What we ordinarily do with these beliefs is deny them – pretend they do not exist. For example, we may state an affirmation, which we know is not completely true ("I am an OK person"). The dialectic process then turns our attention to, and focuses on, what was not said, the opposite that was not included ("There is something wrong with me"). Since we do not want to know this, we have to put our energy into denying it rather than into growth. This keeps the negative expectation alive, though not necessarily in our present awareness.

Shame represents our reaction to denied negative core beliefs. Denial sustains our low-self esteem. Though we deny our negative core beliefs, such as "There is something terribly wrong with me" or "I am unlovable," we actually believe them to be true. Otherwise, we would not work so hard to deny them. Low self-esteem follows awareness of the negative core belief and the fear of it being true. Denial avoids unwelcome agitation.

We need to give up the pretense. When we truly accept our deep belief that the negative expectation is true ("There is something wrong with me"), the dialectic process turns our attention to what is unsaid, the opposite view not included ("There is a lot right with me"). By ending with an affirmation and denying nothing, we release energy to support our self-esteem. We also release ourselves from the dread that our mistaken expectations are the only ways to describe ourselves. When we admit that our negative expectations are not entirely true, we establish the kernel of truth leading to higher self-esteem. We can then proceed to inquire into what has sustained them.

We know that no man lives simply his own life. He lives in great part the lives of his ancestors, of his parents. He lives the lives of his children and the lives of those who are to follow them. He lives but a small part of his life for himself. We do not bury the past because it is within us, but we do modify the past as we live our own lives.
– Ralph Ellison to the graduates of William and Mary College.

> Everything begins on the verge of awareness. The dawn is not and then is. Sleep is and then is not. In between is the awakening
> – George Kimmich Beach

Chapter 14

SLOW AND DETRANCE IMPULSIVE RESPONDING

The response to an event we perceive as compromising our integrity begins with personalizing the threat. This gives rise to an intense discomfort leaving us confused about the event and its aftermath. Overwhelming feelings and disorganized thinking follow and a self-defeating or self-destructive action may be elicited. The reactions following the event comprise the coping impulse trance. The trance hides the shame of our negative beliefs about self. The coping impulse trance also covers the fears we need to face if we are to grow as human beings. Before we can realistically face our fears, we must neutralize the coping impulse trance. This chapter describes how to slow our coping impulses first and subsequently, to detrance them.

"Slowing" and "detrancing" are different terms for a similar process, depending on whether we use three or four steps of the procedure featured in this chapter. "Slowing" uses the first three steps to reduce momentarily the influence of the coping impulse trance. This procedure slows our impulse, but does not go further to help us understand its importance or staying power in our lives.

Detrancing, on the other hand, uses all four steps of the procedure. It helps us to understand the fears that stimulated the coping impulse trance in the first place. Detrancing focuses us on what the impulse did for us. Learning the function of the impulse helps us to accept it as having met our needs in the past and to understand that it no longer fits. Achieving such acceptance diminishes the effect of the coping impulse trance.

The following vignette describes the struggle of Amos who worked on slowing his impulsive reactions to his daughter's dawdling in the morning.

> *Amos is a thirty-six year-old partner in a mid-sized law firm. He and his wife Joan, who is a dietitian, are parents to four-year-old Amy and one-year-old David. After making partner last year, Amos had an early mid-life crisis. He had been so achievement-oriented for so long, that, upon gaining the distinction he had so long craved, he became depressed. Though it sounded so trite to him, he obsessed on the theme, "Is that all there is?" His wife noticed his uncharacteristic moodiness and suggested he seek psychotherapy.*
>
> *One issue that arose in psychotherapy was his distress on the two mornings each week his wife had to get to the hospital by 6:30 AM. His job on those mornings was to wake the children, feed them breakfast, get them dressed, and take them to day care. He*

was also expected in the office for 9:00 AM appointments. In addition to the stress, he was concerned about his involuntary critical comments to his four-year-old daughter Amy. She would dawdle over waking up, dressing, eating her breakfast, or getting ready to travel. He knew it was his problem, but felt he could not control his tongue – "The words just come out." He also saw how easily he became critical of younger people (for example, associates in the firm, tennis partners, nephews and nieces).

His therapist encouraged him to identify mistaken core beliefs corresponding to his overreactions. One belief was a feeling of inadequacy when events did not go his way. Another centered on being "wrong" when disappointed. These statements were too vague to carry much emotional weight for him.

After another morning of conflict with his daughter, Amos arrived disgusted with himself. The therapist asked him what was so terrible about what was happening? Still full of his shame, Amos blurted out, "It means I am a hopeless little shit!" Asked to explain, Amos described his frustration and humiliation as the youngest of three boys. He was goaded and teased by his older brothers. Desperate to be accepted by them but lacking their skill, he would try to keep up with them. Then, he would hear them jeer, "You are hopeless, you little shit."

Amos and his therapist discussed how his "hopeless little shit" belief was seared into *his view of himself. He had long focused on achievement to make that statement invalid. Yet, he feared the shame from any event, like his daughter's dawdling or other perceived disrespect, which would verify its truth. Amos discovered that it was a relief finally to say aloud what the therapist encouraged him to say, "Here I go again. I have the mistaken core belief that I am a hopeless little shit when I am disregarded." It seemed to calm him to say it. Before he left that day, the therapist asked him, "What could you do about your morning crisis that would be self-caring or effective?"*

Unable to respond at the time, Amos agreed to repeat the core belief, "Here I go again ..." when he felt a physical arousal preceding his overreaction. It gave him a moment to reflect and calm himself. It was not until several days later that he could answer the therapist's question. He thought, what he needed to do was so simple, why hadn't he thought of it before? He could arrange things the night before (like his wife did) to reduce the morning pressure. That would leave him some time to give his daughter the attention she needed. Some weeks later, after he found his new plan working he also discovered that he was lowering his unrealistic expectations of others and feeling less critical.

Amos' overreaction to Amy's dawdling was his coping impulse trance. He was equally mindless about his criticism of subordinates. In neither case could he "stop himself." His actions were impulsive. He believed he had to protect himself from feeling inadequate when younger people did not respond pleasantly to his wishes. The work Amos did in psychotherapy revealed two crucial points. First, he identified the negative core belief supporting his impulsive response to perceived disrespect. Second, he discovered an effective way to reduce the power of his coping impulse.

PREPARING FOR THE PROCEDURE

The coping impulse trance is a negative personal ritual stimulated by the confusion following personalizing an event. The four-step sequence substitutes a counter ritual for confusing moments. These steps eventually become so familiar they replace the coping impulse trance. Initially, deliberateness about each step is necessary. Since later steps depend on prior steps, it is also necessary to take them in turn.

The immediate result provides some emotional distance from the threat, so we do not personalize it. This gives us the opportunity to consider acting with our adult skills, choosing how we want to behave rather than acting impulsively. In this way, we concentrate energy on something we *can* do, rather than explain what we cannot do. By focusing on *how* to change, we become focused, clear, and active rather than bored, bewildered, or stuck.

The four steps are based on the idea that we do not *have* to respond immediately when threatened. We always have the right to delay our response or not respond at all based on what is good for *us*. We have the right to choose how and when we *want* to respond, no matter what others think.

The Goal – *Slow or detrance the coping impulse.*

Prerequisites – We are ready to detrance when self-care is practiced regularly and we can tolerate confusion.

The Immediate Problem – We have been acting impulsively for a long time. Feelings of confusion and vulnerability cause discomfort and tempt us to react in the old ways. We need to keep reminding ourselves that reacting to confusing feelings need not be automatic. When confused by anger, for example, we need to remember our tendency has been to avoid or react forcefully. Stopping the urge to act in familiar ways, we need to prepare ourselves to take the time to think before we act. By slowing the coping impulse, we see that we can face our fears.

We are faced with a choice to be effective in our behavior or to act impulsively. We may have no awareness at the time that a choice can be made or what the choice is. Nor do we have any awareness of the self-defeating nature of our impulsive action. I am reminded of a nineteenth century U.S. Senator, Henry Clay, who said, "I would rather be right than president." He ran for president three times and was defeated each time. Rather than learn from his failure, he insisted on his version of "being right." Though his rigidity may have been more political than personal, like many of us with low self-esteem, he may not have had any awareness of how he contributed to his election losses. When we learn to detach ourselves, we can gain the opportunity to choose effective and self-caring behavior.

Revising Our Standards of Success – Effectiveness in slowing impulses may take many repetitions. Therefore, we need to revise our standard of success. Instead of expecting an immediate slowed response to trigger events, define success as anytime we consider the feelings elicited or realize what the feelings are about. At first, it may take hours or even days to be able to consider what happened. Further, it may take many repetitions to get to the point of acting in a way to affect the situation. So, success is *whenever* we are able to act or consider acting in a slowed manner. Moving the response closer to the occurrence of the trigger is described in Diagram # 8.

Some ways to prepare – With the information described below we can prepare ourselves to deal with impulsive actions in a new way.

- *Describe coping impulse sequence* – We identify our coping impulse sequences and review our past history with each type. Then, we describe in detail what happens just before the impulse occurs, as these are the events or circumstances serving as triggers for the impulse. Then, we distinguish the particular bodily discomfort experienced and describe the impulsive behavior in detail. Then, we note exactly how others react to us. Keep a record of when, where, and with whom these impulses occur. We revise the written description according to our experience.

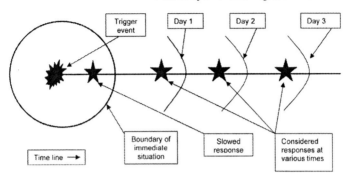

Diagram # 8 – Responding to Trigger Events

- ***Take in feedback*** – Feedback occurs naturally as the result of an event and offers information through our senses. Below are some common ways that we may selectively perceive, block, or distort information coming to us:

  - ☐ <u>Stereotyping</u> – An over-simplified view of a situation based on personally meaningful characteristics;
  - ☐ <u>Fantasizing</u> – An imaginative or inventive view of a situation without regard to the actual circumstances;
  - ☐ <u>Anticipating</u> – Projecting a future view of the situation on to the present;
  - ☐ <u>Projecting</u> – Attributing one's feelings, desires, or beliefs to others;
  - ☐ <u>Past experience</u> – Impressions transferred from similar situations;
  - ☐ <u>Third-party information</u> – Accepting information coming from other people, which may be dubious or inaccurate;
  - ☐ <u>Bias</u> – Preferring certain aspects of a situation, limiting impartial judgment;

☐ <u>Prejudice</u> – Developing beforehand a negative view of a situation or person without regard for real circumstances or personal traits.

These behaviors may protect us from confusion, but they also can warp our experience. Discomfort can result from receiving accurate feedback, but it also provides information and energy for making changes. By taking in feedback from the world around us (from our body and from other people), we identify what in *us* needs attention. Use self-soothing strategies to deal with the discomfort and confusion coming from attention to all this information.

- ***Self-soothing techniques*** – Learn to use these ways of grounding and centering:

  ☐ We *focus* on some aspect of the physical environment: picture the shape, size, and color of nearby objects; focus on the smells and the sounds perceived; or describe what our body touches.

  ☐ <u>Cultivate</u> the habit of *mindfulness*. This allows us to focus our attention on what is happening in the immediate moment rather than focusing on others, the past, or the future. (Be here, now!).

  ☐ We <u>breathe</u> from our diaphragm to calm ourselves. By placing our hands on our stomachs, we can feel it rise on inhaling and fall on exhaling.

- ***Identify core beliefs*** – Core beliefs are the central ideas we have about ourselves. We use them, without awareness, to classify and understand the events in our lives. Since we usually experience a sense of shame on becoming aware of them, they may be difficult to identify. Use these suggestions to start the process:

  ☐ Notice arousal – During and following an event perceived negatively (for example, criticism or rejection), notice the arousal of feeling in your body. Often we feel overwhelmed by the arousal.

  ☐ Use self-soothing option – Upon noticing the arousal, take a deep breath to slow the overreaction and create a bit of emotional distance in which to examine it. Reducing arousal is crucial to permit thinking about the meaning of the current event.

  ☐ Determine event's meaning – Consider that the event is important in some way. We attach special meanings to such events. It is useful to ask ourselves what this event says about us. We may not like this meaning and try to dismiss it. The more objectionable the meaning is to us, the more likely it is an important core belief. The more the belief is phrased in words familiar to a child, the more likely it comes out of our childhood. Denying our mistaken belief is the basis for personalizing the event.

- ***Identify hopeless/helpless scenarios*** – These are the negative core beliefs that tell us we can do nothing about our situation. It is important to surface those beliefs and own them as deeply held but mistaken.

- ***Clarify rewards*** – We get something out of everything we do. It may not seem logical or desirable, but what we do has some type of pay-off for us. Identifying the perceived personal gain associated with the coping impulse will help to understand its real purpose and nature.

- ***Practice relapse prevention*** – Relapse prevention identifies the "red flags" and "dangerous situations" that precede coping impulses and devises alternate strategies to finesse them. Do not expect to do this well each time. The idea is to lessen coping impulses over time. Label each slip a "lapse" rather than a failure or "relapse."

SLOWING AND DETRANCING
(Three and Four Step Procedures)

Impulses occur at a time when it is most difficult to slow them. Using the procedure below anytime *after* an impulsive reaction trains us for the next time we overreact. The self-soothing techniques noted previously help to calm and create the personal distance needed to put these procedures into play. NOTE: The first three steps are used to slow an overreaction while using all four steps is required for detrancing.[35]

---

[35] I am indebted to Naomi A. Serano whose work with the Satir family systems model cued me to this sequence.

Step 1: *Stop and take notice* – Noticing shifts our focus from mindless participation in a process to awareness that "something" is going on. Noticing may be triggered by our body's feedback of physical arousal. Or, another person may note a shift in our non-verbal behavior. By noticing, we get to stand outside ourselves for a moment. This creates some psychological distance, which allows us to slow our response. Since impulses prosper in an atmosphere of mindlessness, noticing the impulse lays the groundwork for an alternate response, but does nothing about what triggered it. Note the temptation to act out of habit instead of choice. Identify bodily reactions, feelings, and thoughts emerging when we do *not* act out of habit.

Familiarity, arousal, cravings, or obsessions can stir noticing. Arousal may result, requiring a relaxation technique for calming. Cravings and obsessions may respond to distraction, relaxation, or centering.

> *Amos noticed the arousal and the irritation welling up inside him when he found his daughter Amy dawdling on getting out of bed, dressing, or eating breakfast. He calmed himself with "belly breathing."*

Step 2: *Acknowledge reaction* – When we name what we have noticed, we actively *express* our recognition of it. We take responsibility for what we observe by *disclosing,* if only to ourselves, our reaction to or our feeling about it. Acknowledgment is active, not passive. It requires that we do something with or make something out of our observation. We face or make contact with the impulse, noting how familiar it is. It is helpful to put the occurrence of the impulse into our own words, by naming it. Verbalizing, "Here I go again" connects current bodily reactions, feelings, and thoughts to the sense of threat felt in the past in similar circumstances. For example, we become aware that the reaction carries a message from our inner selves. The message is in the form of a negative core belief. Acknowledging the message we say, "Here I go again, I have the mistaken belief that I am stupid (or inadequate, or unlovable, etc.)." By verbalizing the awareness rather than passively noticing it, we accept what has been true but which no longer fits.

> *The irritation connected to his core belief. He acknowledged this by saying, "Here I go again; I have the mistaken belief that I am a hopeless little shit."*

Step 3: *Choose a response* – Choosing is a deliberate action. It eliminates some alternatives and responds to others. Choice allows shifting gears from one set of priorities to another. We can respond in terms of our desires, hopes, and plans for the future. We can choose self-care and effective action. By choosing to act in a more functional way, we take a step toward facing our fears. The act of choosing imposes risks. A primary risk is the loss of the benefit gained from the coping impulse. We should expect ambivalence about this loss. Ambivalence is a normal occurrence at such a time. Acting effectively in our own interest challenges the old core belief and affirms a new, more fitting belief.

> *He had a sense of relief following his statement. He could think about his problem with all the skills and resources at his command. The answer was obvious then. Previously, he was*

blinded by the trance and could not see that preparation the night before would free him to give Amy the attention she needed. He felt good but strangely regretful about his discovery.

Step 4: *Accept overreaction* – When we realize how our mistaken core beliefs negatively affect our lives, our first reaction is to want to "get rid" of them. It seems that life would be so much better if they just "went away." This approach, however, fits the old saying of "biting off our nose to spite our face." Core beliefs have had important meaning in our lives. They did something for us at a time when we thought we needed it. So rejecting them is tantamount to rejecting a part of ourselves. Anyway, we cannot do it. It is as good as saying certain experiences we had did not occur.

If rejection is not an option, we accept mistaken core beliefs as a part of us but which no longer fit. Acceptance means ending the denial and recognizing that the beliefs are real. Acceptance does not mean that we approve or disapprove of something but rather that something "is" and "was." I like to use the metaphor of the rain. It does not matter whether we like or dislike the rain. We do not control the rain. The rain is just there. Accepting a mistaken core belief as sustaining a trance reestablishes connections lost long ago among traumatic events. One way of achieving acceptance is to consider what we have learned about what the trance did for us. In this way, we begin to free ourselves of its influence.

"Love me, hate me, but don't ignore me," the saying goes to explain the lengths people will go to excuse abusive actions. Amos saw

that he had protected himself from feeling abandoned by copying the tormentors who suffered his presence but who derided his needs. He did not need to do that anymore.

Chapter 15

DEVELOPING ACTION SKILLS

Our actions convey our belief in our right to choose how we function in the world. Actions reflect the degree of skill, ingenuity, and energy we have developed. They indicate the extent to which we have the personal power to achieve our wants and satisfy our needs.

THREE RESPONSE STYLES

While growing up, we learn three styles for meeting our needs: assertion, submission, and aggression. Each style is necessary for dealing with the variety of our life situations. Submission represents actions which comply with the desires of others and put off meeting our own needs. Aggression involves actions which are self-serving and which disregard the needs of others. Assertive acts display our intent to meet our own needs. Angry outbursts, the abuse of power, and the domination of others are aggressive - not assertive - actions. Assertive acts maintain our integrity and our respect for others.

Submission

Submissive actions are appropriate when we perceive it to be dangerous not to do so. Some ordinary social circumstances (for example, listening to others say their piece, especially when we disagree) call for us to wait our turn. Submissiveness poses problems, however, when it becomes our preferred way of responding. We assume that our rights are subject to the approval of others. Submissive conduct usually seeks to avoid conflict, risky situations, and confusion. It supports dishonest communication by not expressing our thoughts, feelings, and desires clearly. We say "yes" to others when we want to say "no." When being submissive does not work, we find passive-aggressive alternatives, such as withholding, guilt giving, manipulation, or devious alternatives. We gain power submissively through silence or by using such vague language that we are misunderstood.

When we are submissive, we blame ourselves for other's actions. We attempt to calm the situation with apologies or by talking around the point. We agree to do things we really do not want to do. We allow violations of boundaries, denial of rights, and exploitation, coupled with an ignorance of our own needs. This fits a pattern of avoiding conflict and gaining the approval of others. We use "you statements" to avoid self-blame. We assume others should meet our needs. In this way, we evade personal vulnerability and responsibility. A reduced sense of liveliness, loss of self, unsatisfactory relationships, low self-esteem, martyrdom, negativity, disappointment, hurt, and not getting what we want are outcomes of submissiveness.

Aggression

Aggressive actions may be necessary when we have to defend ourselves against clear threats to life or territory. Aggressiveness can become a problem when it is our usual style of responding to others. Aggressive individuals seek to dominate, regardless of the cost. We are aggressive when we express ourselves at the expense of the rights and feelings of others. Aggressive action relies on beliefs that we have to fight for the right to our personal space or satisfaction of our needs. The only way we can see to gain either result is by physical or emotional domination. We direct the resulting hostility at others, especially anyone we perceive to stand in our way.

When we are aggressive we blame or abuse others. Lacking empathy, we violate their boundaries to get what we want. We are impulsive, negative, and mean-spirited. By using "you statements," we blur our fear of domination, dependence, and vulnerability. We protect ourselves by controlling others verbally, by raging, by criticizing, by humiliating others, using put-downs, sarcasm, threat, or physical or sexual violence. Avoidance of responsibility, alienated and strained relationships, negativity, conflict, and hostility are characteristics of the aggressive style.

Assertion

Assertive actions connect our internal experience to actions congruent with our thinking and feeling. Assertion relies on our belief in our right to have and to express our own thoughts, feelings, and desires. It reflects our skill, ingenuity, and energy to protect our personal space and sense of identity against the intrusions of others. We manage our environment for the purpose of meeting our needs. Contrary to popular belief, angry outbursts, the abuse of power, and the domination of others are *not* assertive actions. Assertion requires learning skills, such as the following. Assertive people:

- Express themselves in an emotionally honest way, directly revealing ownership of their feelings and needs when deemed appropriate through the use of first person statements (these are called "I statements");
- Are clear about their connection with and detachment from others (they can calmly say "no" in refusals);
- Do not compromise their own dignity or integrity or that of others;
- Take the feelings of others into account, and let them know they are heard;
- Are able to deal with compliments or criticisms as pleasing or useful information;
- Are open to feedback and learning;
- Accept the reality of their vulnerability, their need to maintain boundaries, and to know themselves;
- Assume and accept that people have different ways of satisfying their needs;
- Understand that differences and conflict between people are inevitable and that compromise is necessary; and
- Have listening, problem-solving, and mediation skills. They can meet their needs without resorting to manipulation, domination, or denying the needs of others.

The consequence of assertive acts is the sense of being "in charge" of one's own life, positive self-esteem, reduced anxiety, and more fulfilling relationships, regardless of whether we get what we want all the time. No one is always assertive nor would that be appropriate. The question is whether we choose to be assertive when it is appropriate to be so.

SKILLS UNDERLYING ASSERTION

Assertiveness is an expression of self-control. It involves knowing what we want, believing in our right to want it, and finding a way to get it without requiring that we always have our way. Likewise, when we do not want something, we can say "no," protect ourselves, and detach from over involvement in the situation.

While saying "no" and "yes" are essential skills, most of us live in a context in which others' needs may conflict or compete with our own. While it is important to assert ourselves and maintain our personal boundaries, we also need to find ways to blend these actions with respect for others. Detachment and empathy skills are crucial in this regard, as they permit us to separate ourselves emotionally yet put ourselves in another person's shoes.

Detachment

Detachment involves the ability to separate oneself emotionally from others. Detaching represents an ongoing recognition of the difference between "I" and "you," the willingness and ability to say "no" when others intrude on our personal space, and recognizing our unique needs, which may differ from others with whom we are personally involved. Detaching from others requires:

- Appreciating that our experience of events differs from that of others;
- Accepting these differences;
- Knowing our limits, maintaining them against self-abuse and abuse by others;

- Knowing our own needs and acting responsibly to meet them by pleasing ourselves;
- Maintaining clarity about how we are different from others and how they differ from us;
- Understanding the power of projection (for example) –
  When others talk about us, they are telling us about themselves;
   What we especially dislike about others, we fear in ourselves;
- Valuing learning over perfection; and
- Understanding that we all make a contribution to all the situations in which we are involved.

Empathy

Empathy involves the ability to view situations from the vantage point of another person. To do so we detach ourselves momentarily from our own needs and listen carefully to what the other person says (and does not say). We observe relevant body language and the surroundings (for example, other people, prior remarks, noise, light, background, etc.). When we listen so well that we can report back to the speaker the sense of what he or she has said or meant without interpretation or distortion, we are demonstrating empathy.

A major barrier to good listening is thinking we already are good listeners. Listening requires practice and feedback. People learn that listening requires attentiveness to others and putting on the back burner thoughts of how to respond. By listening we can know where the other person is "coming from." When we share such understanding, the other person feels heard and respected. By knowing when to detach and when to empathize, we are in a position to assert ourselves appropriately and are more likely to get what we want.

The following example of a negotiation between Mary and Bill (See Chapter 4) relies on the development of mutual empathy. Active listening, mutual respect for each other's position, and narrowing the topic to be discussed are three preconditions for empathic problem solving. The discussion begins as Mary and Bill agree to focus on their anger toward each other. It continues with each partner expressing his or her heartfelt concern. Each responds by sharing their understanding of what the other has said.

> *Mary's anger comes from feeling abandoned by Bill's denial of responsibility for the family and the energy he puts into friends and work. Bill's anger is expressed mainly by his boredom at home since the birth of their first child when "all" of Mary's energy went into the children. They both were scared that they were repeating their parents' pattern of a raging mother and work-a-holic and passive father but did not know what to do about it.*

As their understanding of the basis for each other's anger becomes clear, they move to discuss the underlying yearnings that differently motivate their anger. They make sure the statement is an accurate reflection of what each partner wants. As a result, they begin to become less defensive and move closer emotionally.

> *Mary heard that Bill's hope involved a renewal of their former closeness. Bill heard that*

> *Mary's yearning involved an emotional bond that included their children. Mary and Bill were energized by the renewed hope they saw for their relationship.*

As they reflect on their hopes, they consider their own contribution to the miscommunication.

> *Mary became aware that the loss of her hope of a close family life angered her, much as her mother had been angered. She needed to view her anger as being based in disappointment. Bill became aware that, like his father, he was disappointed that he no longer was "number 1" in his wife's affection, so he put energy into life outside the family, but he was angry with that.*

Their empathic communication has reduced their defensiveness and prepared them to move toward a compromise.

> *Mary recognized that if she could give up being responsible for everything, she could learn to be more inventive about including Bill in the life of the family and to make time for her relationship with him. Then she could get the love and support she needed. Bill had heard that Mary really cared for him. He realized that he did not have to be number 1 to be loved, but he would have to join them.*

This vignette naturally leaves out the tirades and defensiveness that tend to characterize the early stages of this type of negotiation between partners stuck in anger and disappointment. It does reflect the vital steps of an empathetic process.

DANCE LIKE NO ONE IS WATCHING[36]

There is no path to happiness.
Happiness is the path.
So, treasure each moment that you have.

We should work like we don't need the
money.
We should love like we've never been hurt.
We should dance like no one's watching.

[36] (Author unknown)

Stanley J.Gross, Ed. D.

PART V

Not a different person, but more of who I really am.

TRANSFORMATION

We are now ready to explore Level ❺. Though we may still be a bit confused at times, we have heightened access to our inner resources to see us through. We are able to deal with stressful circumstances with increasing competence as a result of our active participation in self-care and our ability to slow our coping impulse trance

The task of transformation is described in Chapter 16. Here is where we exchange our negative and pessimistic view of ourselves for one that is positive and affirming. We can do this as the consequence of forgiving ourselves. We restore the lost historical connections between the abuse/neglect we experienced as children and our mistaken negative core beliefs. This does not happen overnight but as the result of a sustained process of facing our fears and learning about our grief over the loss of childhood. As we work at this process, we will be able to see our increases in skill.

- <u>Our impulsive actions are largely replaced by unrehearsed and appropriate responses</u>.

Since we do not need to control people, places, and things, our self-control anchors a growing spontaneity.

- <u>Access to our needs will be heightened by our awareness of feelings in our body and knowing what they are about</u>. We accept our feelings as a normal part of our lives. Feelings give us information to help us live fully.

- <u>Our thought processes are flexibly attuned to our needs and our goals</u>. We are able to consider varied choices of action in terms of what we want to accomplish.

- <u>Our self-caring actions have us making choices that allow us to value self</u>. We are comfortable in sharing assistance, affection, intimacy, and vulnerability in appropriate ways with chosen others.

- <u>Our degree of self-control allows us to be assertive</u>. Our actions combine a clear valuing of our needs with being sensitive to the needs of others.

- <u>We are comfortable with being receptive to others with whom we are involved</u>. Our openness allows us to be attuned to the dynamics of social situations and empathic in receiving others.

> Forgiveness is giving up all hope of a better past.
> – Anonymous, quoted in the *Boston Globe,* 11/28/99

Chapter 16

GRIEVE THE LOSS OF CHILDHOOD

The work we have done to maintain sobriety, sustain self-care, and slow coping impulses now pays off. We have restored our sense of hope. Relying now on inner controls, we feel safe in our skins. We have the skills and appreciations to restore lost connections to our childhood traumas. Now able to slow our reactivity, we move toward facing our fears and grief about our lost childhood.

The goal – *Regain choice of action by resolving grief over the loss of childhood. We are able to reconnect our actions, feelings, and expectations to each other and to the historic context of childhood abuse and/or neglect.*

Prerequisite – Before we are ready to resolve our grief, sufficient personal growth needs to have occurred for us to feel safe enough to tolerate some confusion. Maintaining self-care and being able to slow impulsive action are indicators of readiness.

The Immediate Problem – Grief holds us in a trance which provokes us to overreact in certain stressful situations. The trance blocks our sadness over the loss of childhood, our anger about the violation of our integrity, and our fear of a loss of self (all of which derive from our childhood fear of abandonment). To break the power of this trance, we need to face as adults the feelings that terrorized us as children.

The Opportunity — Every day our impulsive actions present us with opportunities to reconnect to our childhood trauma. We ordinarily avoid the memory of the trauma for fear of overwhelming feelings lurking just below the surface about the loss of self. We have seen that these feelings emerge in the form of the coping impulse trance. Every time we overreact, we expose ourselves to the disconnection from that early trauma.

Each coping impulse trance represents our attempt to work out in the present what we could not in our family. The overreaction continues to occur because we have not completed processing the overwhelming stressful events that took place when we were children. Access to the blocked connection is difficult. We are unsure that we can face the intense feelings, which we fear will erupt. We do not know that they can never be as frightening as they once were. We do not know that we now have skills and resources we did not have as children. We do not consider that we now have a voice that we did not have as a child.

OVERVIEW OF TASKS

The grief process is presented here in five stages: Denial, Ownership, Facing Feelings, Processing, and Transformation. The separation of these stages is clearer in this writing than in life. Progress through these stages may follow an irregular course according to each person's inner logic. Yet, it is useful to have a framework in which to understand how the transformation takes place as we approach, feel, accept, and resolve our grief. The following overview uses excerpts from the Amos' vignette.

Overcome Denial. Confront our overreactions for what they are – self-destructive responses to current stressors which block emotional development.

> *His depression got Amos into psychotherapy, but it took awhile for him to take responsibility for his problem. That he took his irritation out on his daughter and that it seemed to him so familiar and so unfair eventually helped him break through his denial.*

Own Our Impulsive Reactions to Stressful Events and Their Basis. Although we are not responsible for what happened to us in the past, we are responsible for our behavior now. We recognize this by tolerating the confusion that follows slowing our reactions to stressful events. By doing so we genuinely accept responsibility for our lives. This readies us to face the feelings lying dormant since childhood.

> *Amos acknowledged his deep neediness (to be recognized and accepted by his older brothers). It was the source of an irritability that did not fit his life now. He was sad to recognize that the source of his irritation involved how his older brothers treated him and how little his parents knew of it. He had an acute sense of emptiness that remained when his irritation was spent.*

Face The Feelings We Have Been Avoiding. At this point, we are ready to face the feelings lying dormant since childhood. Not all at once but gradually, as it fits for us, we specifically identify our sadness over the loss of our childhood, anger about violations of our integrity, and our fear of loss of self. Each turns out not to be as bad as it once was. We reencounter the feelings and the terrorizing events of our childhood from an adult perspective with all the skills and resources we now have.

> *Amos visualized his sense of emptiness as a bottomless pit. He cried as he placed in the pit his sadness about all the effort he spent to please people instead of doing things that pleased him. He seemed to be able to approach the sadness first. Later, he was able to place his anger in the pit. He was still angry about the teasing, but he was more aware of the neglect of his parents who now seem not to know or care about his life, his wife, or his children. "Damn them," he said. "They are still overwhelmed by life." He reserved his fears for last. He hesitated as he said, "I was so afraid. They did not know I was there. I was afraid they would not miss me if something happened to me."*

Connect Feelings to Events We Could Not Process As Children. Processing connects the core beliefs that direct our dysfunctional behavior to expectations about how we should behave. By reviewing these expectations in their historic context, we can do something we were unable to do as a child: *Connect our fears and needs.* The connection helps us see how much expectations influenced our lives. Later, we can decide which expectations still suit us and which do not.

> *Amos talked about his need to achieve as a way for him to stand out in his family. He thought it would please them. He also connected the "pleasing others" motive to protecting himself from feeling so needy.*

Connect Our Expectations to Their Related Feelings and Actions. Transformation occurs when we connect our expectations to their related feelings and actions. Tolerating our ambivalence and pain about giving up what we previously treasured allows us to accept our sorrow as something that "happened to happen." This puts us in a position to forgive our caretakers by letting go of our need to have them change the past. Then, we can move on to construct a new reality for ourselves.

> *Amos saw how his irritation was only directed toward those who were vulnerable – much like his older brothers treated him. He also saw how his need to achieve had propelled him into a high stress career where he was rewarded for not taking care of himself or enjoying his life with his wife and children. He also saw that it was he who was now doing this to himself and others. There was no one else responsible. He needed to do some thinking about how he wanted to live his life. This brought him to see and accept that he had created an overwhelming situation, much like his own parents faced. They had done that to themselves. He was not responsible for that,*

> *they were. What he was responsible for was his life.*

DENIAL STAGE

In Denial We Hold On to a Disconnected Past.

- We hold stressful events in an "I'm not there" grief trance which reproduces, without our awareness, self-defeating or self-destructive coping behavior cut off from the historic context of abuse/neglect.

- We have a limited belief in our ability to cope – coping skills are insufficient, and we lose control in an overreaction to stressful experience, confirming a sense of helplessness and futility.

- Overreaction to stressful events is familiar, comfortable, and survival oriented, so anything else seems unsafe or disloyal.

- Confusion from current stressful experience replicates overwhelming childhood reactions to abuse/neglect.

- Questioning the past means confronting the fear of unresolved feelings.

When in denial, we are unwilling or unable to get beyond our repetitive overreactions. We keep personalizing the same old stresses. We may have made a commitment to self-care. We may even have slowed many of the coping impulses in our life, but we are reluctant to face our grief. Whenever we get close to our past, it feels too painful. We experience acute discomfort, confusion, and, sometimes, a craving to return to addictive coping strategies. We may blame or placate. We may experience depression or anxiety and hold on to the expectations that have invisibly ruled our behavior without our awareness for as long as we can remember.

When in the denial stage, we are reluctant to question the past. Though not remembering much of our childhood, we may think of it as happy and view our parents, despite their faults, as blameless. Many of us are quite loyal to this positive vision of our family. We express the positive in various ways. We believe in the family rules. We are defensive about our core beliefs. Life roles are interpreted in inflexible ways.

Our overreaction – the coping impulse – is the surface manifestation of our habitual attempt to work out in the present what we did not work out in our family. We repeat these reactions in our old dysfunctional way, so they have the same result. The way we respond to criticism or abuse, for example, parallels the way we responded to criticism or abuse when we were children. Criticism and abuse confused us then; they confuse us now. We feared confusion then; we fear it now. We avoided the fear then; we avoid it now. The specific ways of avoiding fear and confusion may have changed over the years, but our goal has not changed. We remain super-sensitive to criticism or abuse because we have never faced the fear they engender. In this way, we have the opportunity, over and over again, to face as adults what we were unable to face as children. As long as we keep doing what we did in the past, we will not put the issue behind us.

OWNERSHIP STAGE

Ownership Means Confronting the Denial. Tasks of Preparation Are:

- Become selective about which issues require confrontation at a particular time.

- Acknowledge that the abuse/neglect occurred, but accept we could not be responsible for what happened to us as children. We are responsible, though, for making changes in the present. We are the only ones who can.

- Acknowledge our impulsive response to current stressful events.

- Acknowledge the contribution we make to our current overreactions by:
    Being afraid to face our unresolved feelings;
    Maintaining the victim role; and
    Personalizing current stress.

- Acknowledge that no one makes us do what we do and that our overreaction is useful to us in survival and maintaining familiarity and comfort.

- Create safety so the confusion from the arousal and distressing feelings is countered by acknowledging the ambivalence and self-soothing.

- Create detachment by saying, "Here I go again," when stressful experience occurs.

- Reach out to others in order to talk about your struggle.

Ownership involves being selective about the emotional issues we are ready to confront. We neither can expect to confront all outstanding emotional issues nor confront issues about which we feel unsafe. Selectivity involves developing a degree of safety that we provide for ourselves. We acknowledge that we are apprehensive when facing our fears. Owning the fear permits us to normalize it, thus reducing its power.

We can go on to acknowledge that we are the only ones who can change things for ourselves. By doing so, we take responsibility for our own lives. Though we are not responsible for what happened to us when we were children, we are responsible *now* for doing something about the challenges we face. No one else can change things for us. Waiting for others to change, pleading, feeling hopeless or helpless, or looking for magic, all avoid the daily work that it takes to raise self-esteem.

To own responsibility means knowing we make a contribution to all the events we are a part of. It is as Pogo[37] said, "We have met the enemy, and he is us." In this way, we recognize that the only one we control is ourselves. This may mean, for example, becoming aware of how we have not been self-caring and deciding that self-care has priority. Taking responsibility for our overreactions and pain moves us beyond victimization to ownership of our behavior. We acknowledge that it is we, not others, who are overreacting to current events.

[37] Comic book possum (circa 1960s) and resident of the Okefenokee (FL) Swamp.

By *owning* who we are, we step on the path to *being* who we are. This, however, is easier said than done. Owning who we are requires self-awareness, yet our awareness is often missing and incomplete. We have come to distrust the inner voice that has led us to overreact in the past. It seems we go around in circles. What do we own? Looking at ourselves seems to make things worse in the present, evoking pain and shame rather than good feelings about ourselves. Must there be pain to grow?

The bad news is: it can be uncomfortable when we are aware of our painful and negative view of ourselves. The good news is: it is survivable and less difficult to deal with than we fear. We know more than we think we do, and we are stronger than we think we are. Believing this, we acquire an essential ingredient for growth – the willingness to tolerate some discomfort and confusion. We create a sense of safety to stay with the confusion rather than personalize stressful events. Thus, we reduce our anxiety and create a supportive context that affirms the trauma or neglect and fires the hope to increase self-esteem.

To discover what to own, we look at what we want to hide from others. A pundit said, "Honor the source: What we deny the most is what we really are." Criticism, conflict, rejection, intimidation, and failure are hard to take. They stimulate dread, grief, embarrassment, shame, guilt, uncertainty, confusion, or loss of control. Denial may also involve frustration, tenseness, anxiety, or depression and physical symptoms of grief such as fatigue or insomnia. These reactions, which make us feel the most vulnerable and to which we attach shame, are also the most essential to explore.

Hiding these reactions from others and ourselves, we maintain the very state of low self-esteem we say we want to improve. We lead a double life – divided between who we are and who we pretend to be (and fooling ourselves more than anyone else). Silence is a shield and source of power as long as we believe it helps us to avoid the public consequences of what we have been hiding. However, it also isolates us and stimulates guilt about behaving in a fraudulent way. Silence maintains our low self-esteem. We feel undeserving of any success or fraudulent when we do succeed. Naming our reaction makes a difference by reducing the strain that comes from denial and elicits validation by having a new identity replace a lurking fear.

Challenging the impulse, as we have in slowing it down, ultimately means we take responsibility for it. We own it as *ours*. It is *our* way of responding. "Here I go again." No longer does anyone *make* us respond that way. We learned to respond in that way because it was useful for us to do so. We have felt more comfortable, and it has been more familiar to do so than do anything else! Our self-destructive or self-defeating behavior has had value to us. By identifying the value, we accept that the abuse/neglect in our childhood really did happen to us and that it did stimulate our coping impulses. It does not matter whether we like this. Acceptance is not about agreeing or disagreeing. It is about acknowledging a reality that exists, like it or not.

FACING FEELINGS STAGE

FACING FEELINGS is Essential. Genuine Feelings Touch on Our Deepest Yearnings and Hold Messages about Our Needs. The Tasks of Experiencing Grief Are:

- Acknowledging that we now have skills and resources we did not have as children, so facing our unresolved feelings cannot be as bad as it was.

- Opening to the feelings held by the grief.

- Experiencing our grief:
  To connect us to childhood deprivations; and
  To reconnect us to our feelings, which are separated from the childhood experience of abuse/neglect.

- Facing our grief means confronting ideas, images, and terrors associated with childhood events of abuse/neglect.

- Re-exposing ourselves to distressing feelings that we could not process at the time, Such as:
  Sadness about the loss of childhood;
  Anger about:
    The violation of our childhood integrity;
    Not being protected; and
    Not having anyone available to process our feelings;
  Fear about being abandoned by our caretakers.

Preparing to face our feelings includes tolerating the physical and emotional arousal associated with stressful events. Though the confusion we feel at this point is inevitable, it need not be overwhelming. What makes it overwhelming is its association with a time in our childhood when we did not have the skills, resources, or outside support we have today. Now, with our adult abilities and resources available, these feelings can never be as bad again as they once were. Knowing this, we may stay with facing our feelings rather than retreat into coping impulses.

We need to acknowledge the feelings we have had difficulty facing. We are sad about the loss of our childhood. We are angry about the abuse and neglect we experienced and about our childhood being taken from us. We fear a loss of self, prompted by a sense of abandonment by our childhood caretakers. By admitting these feelings we open ourselves to re-experience them. We face the abusive and neglectful events of our childhood – events that overwhelmed our limited emotional capacity when we were children. The difference now is that we do it from an adult perspective. We are empowered by the skills and access to resources we have acquired.

Facing our feelings allows us to discover vital information unavailable elsewhere. Feelings contain information about how we perceive our life situations. This information, being unique to us, is essential to self-understanding. It also tells us how we came to define the circumstance as a problem.

Mourning begins as we allow ourselves to experience and verbalize our pain. The pain results from our deep sadness over the loss of our childhood; our intense anger about our childhood being taken from us; and the abandonment we feared unless we followed the wishes of our caretakers. It is crucial to allow ourselves to feel these feelings fully. The vague picture we have had about our childhood fills in with more detail as we experience these feelings and to what they refer. These feelings connect to the deprivation of our emotional needs. We yearn to have our needs satisfied. Mourning allows us to re-experience the losses associated with the need deprivation. Then, we can process them to reconnect our feelings, thoughts, and actions to their historic context.

Imagine this scene: three to four hundred people, strangers to each other, are told to pair up and ask their partner one single question, "What do you want?" over and over and over again. Could anything be simpler? One innocent question and its answer. And yet, time after time, I have seen this group exercise evoke unexpectedly powerful feelings. Often, within minutes, the room rocks with emotion. Men and women – and these are by no means desperate or needy but successful, well-functioning, well-dressed people who glitter as they walk – are stirred to their depths. They call out to those who are forever lost – dead or absent parents, spouses, children, friends: "I want to see you again." "I want your love." "I want to know you're proud of me." "I want you to know I love you and how sorry I am I never told you." "I want you back – I am so lonely." "I want the childhood I never had." "I want to be healthy – to be young again. I want to be loved, to be respected. I want to matter, to be important, to be remembered."

– Irvin D. Yalom, *Love's Executioner*, (p. ix)

Tolerating the physical and emotional arousal, we face the feelings. When we do, we ready ourselves to process events we were unable to talk about as children. As our feelings gain a visible expression, we see them connect to particular thoughts, which, in turn, open the door to examine events and reactions occurring in our childhood.

PROCESSING STAGE

PROCESSING Abuse/Neglect Did Not Occur Earlier. Others Can Now Help Us to Review, Reevaluate, and Rework Our Experience. The Tasks of Processing Are:

- To clarify expectations (roles, rules, and core beliefs) by reviewing messages and need deprivations affecting current behavior.

- To connect feelings, thoughts, and actions associated with overreactions to their historic contexts.

- To identify current emotional needs.

- To assess expectations for what no longer fits.

- To consider what needs changing.

Processing is the act of reviewing our experience. We process with the purpose of deliberately connecting our feelings, thoughts, and actions to their historic context. Once we genuinely accept our feelings and allow ourselves to experience them, processing helps us to learn about their connections to our emotional needs. As we allow ourselves to receive these messages, we become aware of the expectations invisibly influencing our behavior. Making them explicit is the goal of this stage. Lurking on the edge of awareness, these expectations have great influence because of their invisibility. Once they are out in the open, we can determine their relevance. Then, we can deal with them on their merits. Reviewing these expectations in their historic context is the goal of processing at this point. We are, then able to choose which expectations still fit and which require revision.

Our inability to talk about trauma at the time it occurred makes it influential in our later development. When a disaster occurs in our society, we usually rush in with counselors to help victims debrief the experience. By helping victims to process their horror and sense of responsibility for it, we hope to prevent it from entering memory in this unrefined state. So, we encourage trauma victims to share their feelings about their experience. We give them support. We tell them they are responding normally to an abnormal situation. We insist they are not responsible for what happened to them.

This is not what usually happens when children are abused or neglected. The abuse may go on and on for years and never be processed. It goes into memory unrefined. Since children see themselves as the centers of the universe and responsible for everything that happens within it, they misperceive it. They believe they are responsible for being abused and neglected. Misperceiving their responsibility, they victimize themselves. Their lifetime of self-defeating and self-destructive actions represents a continuing re-victimization of themselves. Their coping impulse trances and insufficient skills maintain a condition that punishes them for something for which they could not be responsible.

This is why we talk about it now. Through sharing our feelings and beliefs we get to face them. Thus, we get to see that most do not fit the life we have made for ourselves today. They belong to an earlier time when we believed what we had to believe or suffer the most dreadful consequences. Once we appreciate the service these beliefs did for us in that distant past, we can come to see they no longer are much use to us now. They can be put on a shelf. This way, we know we can return to them, if we need to, but, for the most part, we can safely ignore them. Since this is so, we can now forgive ourselves.

> You couldn't exorcise the past either by returning to it or by running away. You couldn't resolve to put it out of your mind and memory, because it was part of your mind and memory. You couldn't reject it because it had made you what you were. It had to be remembered, thought about, accepted, perhaps even given thanks for, since it had taught her how to survive.
> – P.D. James, *A Certain Justice.*

TRANSFORMATION STAGE

TRANSFORMATION Involves Accepting, Letting Go, Forgiving, and Moving On. The Tasks of Transformation Are:

- Accepting our anger at our caretakers to relieve us of responsibility for their abuse/ neglect and to permit us to give up the hope that they return our childhood to us.

- Letting go of:
  Our sorrow over the childhood we missed;
  Our anger at our caretakers for their abuse/neglect; and
  Our fear of abandonment and loss of self.

- Viewing the abuse/neglect as something that "happened to happen" and no longer needs to define us.

- Acknowledging and tolerating the ambivalence we have about giving up the familiar survival-oriented protection that we have allowed to define ourselves.

- Forgiving our caretakers by transferring to them the responsibility for the consequences of their abuse/neglect.

- Acknowledging what we have learned from our experience, especially the strengths we demonstrate as survivors.

- Accepting our emerging feelings about ourselves as OK: our energy, comfort with self, hopefulness, and effectiveness.

- Moving on to construct a new reality by changing the expectations that no longer fit.

Transformation is the end result of our mourning. It occurs as we accept our losses; let go of our anger and fear; forgive our caretakers; and move on. It is, however, not something that we can directly make happen. Rather, it is something we let happen as a result of participating fully in the mourning process.

Our anger about our childhood victimization is the final logjam blocking transformation. Often, we block experiencing the anger with a misguided loyalty to our parents. We fear the pain of dammed-up feelings or get lost in a generalized bitterness. The basis for the blocked anger is the denial of the ancient hope that our parents will change the past and provide what we missed in childhood. Maintaining that hope and the attendant hunger for withheld emotional support are essential factors in not getting on with our lives.

The first step in freeing ourselves involves awareness of our anger about being cheated of our childhood by our parents and believing the anger legitimate. Experiencing our feelings allows us to process them in terms of their historic contexts and clarify the expectations that developed. Then, we can accept that our caretakers were unable to give us what we needed, including sufficient protection. *This was not our fault!* Instead of blaming ourselves for what happened to us, we need to accept the reality of the abuse or neglect as something that unfortunately happened *to us.* The responsibility for it belongs to our parents, whether it was intentional or not. Even if our parents now asked for our forgiveness for the abuse or neglect they perpetrated when we were children, it would not change it. Nothing can change the past. This means we can let go of the primal wish to have our parents change our history of abuse and neglect.

> I now believe, however tentatively, that my quest for a new and improved childhood is tantamount to a wish to die, to stop the world and get off. The nurturing womb I've been searching for simply isn't out there . . . . The time for that absolute care taking is past, and if I didn't get it forty years ago, I'm not going to get it now, no matter how implacably I insist on it.
> – Daphne Merken, "The Black Season," The New Yorker, January 8, 2001, p. 39.

Accepting our right to be angry, we free ourselves of responsibility for what was not our doing. It is, then, placed where it rightly belongs. This prepares the way for forgiving our parents. Forgiveness is based on an understanding of how things really happened. It returns to them the responsibility for their own actions. In forgiveness, we can understand how they too were probably the targets of abuse or neglect but they could not free themselves from the cycle of dysfunction. That is their problem. Now, we can find ways to be responsible for ourselves.

Approaching change, we acknowledge our ambivalence. We have to give up the way we have understood the world. Though our actions may be self-defeating or self-destructive, they are a known quantity. They are "our way." Our actions are central to our definition of "who we are." To give up an action means allowing something new to develop with all the attendant confusion and vulnerability. Yet, the prospect of change offers us the relief of a burden. The very thought excites us and gives us hope. Tolerating this ambivalence, cherishing how we defined ourselves, appreciating the strength we manifested in surviving, and knowing we can always return to our dysfunctional ways, we open ourselves to pursuing a new and more functional way of approaching life.

Constructing our new reality includes changing the expectations that previously gave meaning to our behavior. In a conscious process over time, we review and change the rules, roles, and core beliefs that have been part of our old way of reacting. As we become successful in doing so, we will experience subtle changes that tell us we are moving on the road to positive self-esteem. R. S. Weiss[38] described these goals:

- Ability to give energy to everyday life.
- Psychological comfort, as demonstrated by freedom from pain and distress.
- Ability to experience gratification – to feel pleasure when desirable, hoped for, or enriching events occur.
- Hopefulness regarding the future, being able to plan and care about plans.
- Ability to function with reasonable adequacy in social roles as spouse, parent, and member of the community.

Transformation has an emergent quality, containing all that is new as well as all that is old but combined into a new oneness. The English mystery novelist P.D. James

---

[38] Weiss, R.S. (1988). Loss and Recovery. *Journal of Social Issues, 44* (3). 44.

has her character Kate Miskin in *Original Sin* arriving at this point in her life. Being in her grandmother's apartment symbolized for Kate the pain of living in squalid and deteriorating surroundings as well as the unacknowledged love she felt for her uncomplaining caretaker. She vowed:

> *"When I'm grown up I shall get out of this. I shall leave bloody Ellison Fairwether Buildings forever. I shall never come back again. I shall never be poor again. I shall never have to smell this place again."*

> *She had chosen the police service through which to make her escape, resisting the temptation to enter the sixth form or try for university, anxious only to begin earning, to get away. That first Victorian flat in Holland Park had been the beginning. After her grandmother's death she had stayed on for nine months, knowing that to leave at once would be a desertion, although she was not sure from what, perhaps from a reality that had to be faced, knowing too that there was expiation to be made, things she had to learn about herself, and that this was the place in which to learn them. The time would come when it would be right to leave and she could close the door with a sense of completion, of putting behind a past which couldn't be altered, but which could be accepted with its miseries, its horrors – yes, and its joys – reconciled and made part of herself.*[39]

[39] James, P.D. (1994). *Original Sin*. NY: Knopf. p.114.

When we reach the end of our arduous journey, we know it, because we will have recreated ourselves in our own image. Our empowered self is the "old us" enhanced by all the growth we have experienced. We are not someone "brand new," but we are more open to change; more tolerant of confusion; and ready to deal with the demands of an uncertain future. We also see that the journey of increasing self-esteem never ends. After all, the world keeps changing, new experiences offer themselves, stress occurs, and there are challenges to meet and problems to solve. Our actions may even be dysfunctional in some of these situations. The difference will be that, in using our new skills and intuition, we are able to *choose* to meet our needs rather than overreact in the old automatic way.

Stanley J.Gross, Ed. D.

A Self-Esteem Reading List

Baldwin, M. & Satir, V. (1983). *Satir: Step By Step*. Palo Alto, CA: Science and Behavior Books.

Baumeister, R. F. (1993). *Self-esteem: The Puzzle of Low Self-Regard.* NY: Plenum.

Bednar, R.L., Wells, M.G., & Peterson, S.R. (1989). *Self-Esteem: Paradoxes and Innovation in Clinical Theory and Practice*. Washington, DC: American Psychological Association.

Benson, H & Proctor, W (2003). *The Break-Out Principle*. NY: Scribner.

Brown, S. (1992). *Safe Passage: Recovery for Adult Children of Alcoholics.* NY: Wiley.

Brown, S. & Lewis, V. (1999). *The alcoholic family in recovery*. NY: Guilford.

Coopersmith, S. (1967). *Antecedents of Self-Esteem*. San Francisco: Freeman.

Csikszentmihalyi, M. (1990). *Flow: The Psychology of Optimal Experience*. NY: Harper & Row.

De Becker, G. (1997). *The Gift of Fear*. NY: Random House.

Domar, A.D. & Dreher, H. (2000). *Self-Nurture.* NY: Viking.

Duhl, B. (1983). *From the Inside Out and Other Metaphors.* New York, NY: Brunner/Mazel.

Englander-Golden, P. & Satir, V., (1990). *Say It Straight: From Compulsions to Choices.* Palo Alto, CA: Science and Behavior Books.

Evans, K. & Sullivan, J.M. (1995). *Treating Addicted Survivors of Trauma.* NY: Guilford Press.

Everstine, D.S. & Everstine, L. (1993). *The Trauma Response: Treatment for Emotional Injury.* NY: Norton.

Fennell, Melanie (2001). *Overcoming Low Self-Esteem.* NY: NYU Press.

Firestone, R.W. (1990). *Compassionate Child Rearing: An In-Depth Approach to Optimal Parenting.* NY: Plenum.

Foster, G.D. & Nonas, C.A. (2004). *Managing Obesity: A Clinical Guide.* Chicago: American Dietetic Association.

Frey, D. & Carlock, C.J. (1984). *Enhancing Self-Esteem.* Muncie, IN: Accelerated Development.

Hayes, K.F. (2002). *Move Your Body Tone Your Mind.* Oakland, CA: New Harbinger.

Herman, J. L. (1992). *Trauma and Recovery.* NY: Basic Books.

Hewitt, J.P. (1998). *The Myth of Self-Esteem.* NY: St Martin's Press.

Hillman, C. (1992). *Recovery of Your Self-Esteem: A Guide for Women.* NY: Simon & Shuster

Katz, L.G. (1993). *Distinctions Between Self-Esteem and Narcissism: Implications for Practice.* ERIC/EECE Publication #212.

Kaufman, G. (1991). *Dynamics of power: Fighting Shame and Building Self-Esteem.* Rochester, VT: Schenkman.

Kitchens, J.A. (1991). *Understanding and Treating Codependence.* Englewood Cliffs, NJ: Prentice-Hall.

Langer, E. J. (1989). *Mindfulness.* Reading, MA: Addison-Wesley.

Linehan, M. (1993). *Cognitive-Behavioral Treatment of Borderline Personality Disorder.* NY: Guilford.

McKay, M. & Fanning, P. (1987). *Self-Esteem: The Ultimate Program for Self-Help.* NY: MJF Books.

Mellin, L. (1998). *The Diet-Free Solution.* NY: Regan Books.

Miller, A. (1984). *For Your Own Good: Hidden Cruelty in Child Rearing and the Roots of Violence.* NY: Farrar, Straus, Giroux.

Nelson, M. E. (1997). *Strong Women Live Longer.* NY: Ballentine Books.

Nelson, M. E., Baker, K.R., and Roubenoff, R. (2002). *Strong Women and Men Beat Arthritis.* NY: G. P. Putnam's Sons.

Nerin, B. (1985). *Family Reconstruction: Long Day's Journey Into Light.* NY: Norton.

Nerin, W.F. (1993). *You Can't Grow Up Till You Go Back Home.* Gig Harbor, WA: Magic Mountain Publishing Company.

Paine-Gernee, K. (1990). *Emotional Healing: A Program for Emotional Sobriety.* NY: Warner.

Pope, A.W., McHale, S.M., & Craighead, W.E. (1988). *Self-Esteem Enhancement with Children and Adolescents.* Boston: Allyn & Bacon.

Prochaska, J.O., Norcross, J.C., & DiClemente, C.C. (1994). *Changing for Good.* NY: Avon Books.

Satir, V. (1988). *The New People Making.* Mountain View, CA: Science and Behavior Books.

Satir, V. (1975). *Self-Esteem.* Millbrae, CA: Celestial Arts.

Satir, V., Banmen, J., Gerber, J., & Gamori, M. (1991). *The Satir Model: Family therapy and Beyond.* Palo Alto, CA: Science and Behavior Books.

Schutz, W. (1994). *The Human Element.* San Francisco: Jossey-Bass.

Schwab, J. (*et.al.*) (1989). *The Satir Approach to Communication.* Palo Alto, CA: Science and Behavior Books.

Schwartz, J.M. (1996). *Brain Lock: Free Yourself from Obsessive-Compulsive Behavior.* NY: HarperCollins

Siegleman, E.Y. (1983). *Personal Risk: Mastering Change in Love and Work.* NY: Harper & Row.

Seligman, M.E.P. (1993). *What You Can Change and What You Can't.* NY: Fawcett Columbine.

Sorensen, M.J. (2001). *Low Self-Esteem: Misunderstood & Misdiagnosed.* Sherwood, OR: Wolf.

Sorensen, M.J. (1998). *Breaking the Chain of Low Self-Esteem.* Sherwood, OR: Wolf.

Steffenhagen, R.A. (1990). *Self-Esteem Therapy.* NY: Praeger.

Taffel, R. (1999). Discovering Our Children. *Family Therapy Networker, 23* (5), 24-35.

Trungpa, C. (1991). *Orderly Chaos.* Boston: Shambala.

Twerski, A. (1995). *Life's Too Short: Pull the Plug of Self-Defeating Behavior and Turn on the Power of Self-Esteem.* NY: St. Martin's Griffin.

Wegschieder, S. (1987). *Learning to Love Yourself: Finding Your Self-Worth.* Pompano Beach, FL: Health Communications.

Whitfield, C. L. (1987). *Healing the Child Within: Discovery and Recovery for Adult Children of Dysfunctional Families.* Deerfield Beach, FL: Health Communications.

Willett, Walter C. (2001). *Eat, Drink, and Be Healthy: The Harvard Medical School Guide to Healthy Eating.* NY: Simon & Schuster.

Witt, J.G. & Garner, A. (1990). *Life-Skills for Adult Children.* Deerfield Beach, FL: Health Communications.

Wolinsky, S. & Ryan, M.O. (1991). *Trances People Live: Healing Approaches in Quantum Psychology.* Falls Village, CT: Bramble Company.

About the Author

Stanley J. Gross, **Ed.D.** authored the award winning *Of Foxes and Hen Houses: Licensing and the Health Professions* (Greenwood Press, 1984). He practices as a licensed psychologist in Quincy, MA and is Professor Emeritus of Counseling Psychology, Indiana State University, Terre Haute, IN. His doctorate is from Columbia University. He did post-doctoral work at the University of Illinois Medical School and at the Center for Addictions Study at Harvard Medical School. He also trained with family therapy pioneer Virginia Satir. Dr. Gross regularly offers workshops on self-esteem for the public and for professionals. For more about Dr. Gross and self-esteem visit self-esteempathways.com.